Open Life
The Philosophy of Open Source

to Andy
hope you enjoy this
nice meeting you
MySQL Conference 2012

Henrik Ingo

Translation: Sara Torvalds
Editor: Helen Wire

www.openlife.cc

First published 2005 in Finnish as *Avoin Elämä: Näin toimii Open Source*
This first English language edition published 2006 by Lulu.com
English translation: Sara Torvalds
Editor, English edition: Helen Wire

(cc) 2006 Henrik Ingo

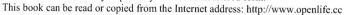
ISBN 978-1-84728-611-6

To order this book online visit **www.openlife.cc** or order it through your local bookstore.

Printed by Otamedia, Finland

Contents

Introduction

I've never figured out why books have introductions – surely, few people ever bother to read them. Often it's pointless stuff, which I tend to skip in favour of always getting to the point as soon as possible. So, when I started writing this book, I decided it wouldn't have an introduction. However, now that it's about to be published I do feel like saying something about how it came to be written. But please don't feel under any obligation to waste your time reading this introduction. My advice is that you leap ahead to the beginning of Part One now, which is what I'd do if I were you.

The idea for this book came to me in the early days of 2003, when I was working as a programming trainer at Tieturi, the Finnish IT training provider. We were organizing a seminar on *Linux and Open Source*, and I was to give a talk on the defining characteristics of the Open Source culture. Since the City of Turku in Finland had just announced that they would start using Linux, we thought people might be interested in such a seminar. However, due to a lack of applicants, the seminar was cancelled, but prior to hearing about that I'd already started preparing my talk by setting up a simple text file called *Open Source philosophy.txt* on my computer at work. In it I kept a bullet-pointed list of ideas or www-links, which eventually evolved into an outline for this book.

Although the seminar itself was dead and buried, the computer file remained and eventually started to live a life of its own. Over time, I added more and more bullet points. I was fascinated by and interested in the culture and working methods of the Open Source community – they were so unlike those of the traditional programming world and, indeed, of any traditional work culture.

It's not that a lot hasn't already been written about Open Source, but rather that the books I had read mostly represented one or other of two camps. If a book is written by somebody inside the Open Source community, the content tends to be difficult for the average person, that is anyone who isn't already fascinated by the detailed history of Linux or the particulars of a given programming language. If, on the other hand, a book has been written by an *outsider* for the benefit of other outsiders, it usually loses some of the honesty and directness, some of the magic of the Open Source attitude – in short, something of the very quality that had always fascinated me about that community. That's why I wanted to write a book that gives a broader view of Open Source than being yet another explanation of *how Linux works in a computer*; to write one that's more about *how Open Source works outside a computer*, drawing on real examples and stories from the history of the Linux and Open Source revolution. My book now has more than sixty stories, or case studies, and I think I've done reasonably well in covering the players who have taken part in the revolution during the first 13 years of Linux. I trust readers will find the examples I have chosen as fascinating as I do.

Writing a book alongside a full-time job is a big undertaking and something I wouldn't want to do again anytime soon. Some 18 months have passed since I finished the first part, and I keep repeating the Linux principle to myself: *It's ready when it's ready.* I have to confess that spouting fine sentiments is a lot easier than living them, and impatience has sometimes almost overtaken me.

The drawn-out writing process has also been a challenge because of the topicality of the subject. In recent years Linux, OpenOffice, Firefox and the other Open Source programs have been making their final breakthroughs and development is incredibly fast. By the time I'd reached the last page, I turned around to discover that Red Hat Linux, which had been Red Hat's main product, was no more; that the second-largest Linux company SuSE had been bought up by Novell; that Mandrake was no longer in liquidation and was making a healthy profit. And as I write this introduction, I find that the recently published Mozilla Firefox is an incredibly sharp browser, which outperforms Internet Explorer in all categories. Only yesterday, Mozilla was criticized in this book for being 'a bit slow'.

Another of my reasons for wanting to write this book was a desire to encourage Open Source thinking outside the IT world, and Part Four is all about that. And now I find that *Wired* magazine has just published a CD on which all the music can be copied freely under the Creative Commons licence. This is not the first such album of music, but this time some relatively well-known names have joined in, such as the Beastie Boys and David Byrne, who had special permission from their record companies to take part. So even in the music field the open revolution is making progress.

Many friends encouraged and helped me during the process of writing this book. Pertti Vehkavuori, in particular, is a champion of encouragement and help, and everybody should have at least one 'Pertti' as a friend. When he'd read the first part, he phoned and spoke to me for an hour about mean-spiritedness in his own work as a physiotherapist and trainer. Having read the second part he then phoned, keen to know when the third part would be finished. Talking to a physiotherapist, who I assume had never knowingly used Linux himself, reassured me that the book was becoming what I'd intended it to be.

This book would not exist without my dear wife Sanna. Many thoughts, including the first part which sets the tone for the book, are based on conversations with her. Also, she made it very clear that she would like to be the wife of an author, which is what made this engineer take seriously the notion of writing a book. Certainly, *Open Life* would never have come to fruition without the innumerable Sundays on which she took over my share of the dishes, laundry and other domestic tasks and left me free to focus on my writing. Oh how I love you, Sanna.

henrik ingo
In Matinkylä, Espoo, on the eve of Finland's Independence Day 2004

Introduction to the English edition

As I observed in the original introduction, writing a book about Open Source business models borders on being impossible. During the year it took me to write *Open Life: The Philosophy of Open Source*, all the major Linux distributions – except stable-as-ever Debian – underwent significant changes. Since publication of the Finnish edition, another year has passed while we prepared this English edition, and the past year has seen just as many changes in the Open Source world as the one before it. Mandrake, one of the four big distributions when the book was being written, has miraculously dwindled to being an insignificant player. While Ubuntu – first heard of just half a year prior to publication of the Finnish book, and therefore not mentioned at all – has rapidly toppled all other contenders for the top spot as favourite desktop distribution, and along the way has generated the most hype.

In the past twelve months, one very positive surprise has been the explosive adoption rate in Creative Commons licensed material available on the Internet. In the first three months alone, after publication of the Finnish edition of *Open Life*, the amount of Creative Commons material indexed by the Yahoo! search engine soared from 16 million to 53 million items.[1] Then there are services like Flickr! that now expressly offer easy usage of Creative Commons sharing of images and other materials.[2] One important Finnish event last year was the release of the full-length sci-fi movie *Star Wreck*, which was made available for free download under a Creative Commons licence, and thanks to this method of distribution it has actually become the most watched Finnish film ever.[3] With millions of viewings, it has even outdone the old World War II movie *Tuntematon sotilas* (*Unknown soldier*).

Since one of my prime motives for writing *Open Life* was to introduce non-programmers to the concept of Open Source and thereby stimulate its use in just such ways, it is truly encouraging to note that, even as I wrote, many such projects were already underway, and the trend is catching on.

---

1   http://creativecommons.org/weblog/entry/5579

2   http://flickr.com/

3   http://www.starwreck.com/

With all these rapid developments and surprise turns, it was important for me to consider whether or not I should update *Open Life* for this English edition. Finally, I decided not to update it (apart from correcting a few errors), but simply to translate the original text. My rationale for this was that developments would be just as vivid this year as they had been in the last two, and by the time the translation was done the content would, again, already have become outdated. Also weighing in on the decision was the sheer volume of work required to update the whole text. Essentially, Part Three would have needed more or less complete revision, and Part Four probably to be partially rethought to encompass the many developments happening in the Open Content field. By the way, since I decided not to update the text for this translation, readers should note that phrases such as 'last year' and 'ten years ago' refer to 2004/03 and 1994/93 respectively.

The only feasible alternative was to accept that this edition of *Open Life* is a snapshot of how things were at the time of writing. Having taken this decision, I've begun to think I may have been quite lucky with the timing of the book, because 2005 was actually a good year to produce such a snapshot. For instance, thanks to broadband, the CD-selling business of Linux distributions is becoming an historical footnote, while 'enterprise distributions' have gained greater prominence. Another example is the Linux kernel development process which kicked into a higher gear with the release of Linux 2.6.0 to accommodate the rising volume and speed of development, and actually abandoning some processes that were in place when this book was being written. In a sense, and quite by chance, I may have captured a snapshot of the Open Source world just as it was about to transform itself into something newer, bigger and completely different, and if this is true *Open Life* may also serve to document for history the first 10–15 years of Linux and Open Source development, or counting from the genesis of the GNU project, the first 20 years.

Naturally, I was often tempted to make a minor *adjustment* here and there. For instance, it seems I once thought Bruce Perens' UserLinux project was important enough to deserve a mention. At the time of writing, I must have seen a bright future for this project that never made a single tangible product. Although Firefox is mentioned in the Mozilla story, its success is only anticipated, not yet a fact. That, together with having no mention of Ubuntu, makes me wonder, could all of that have been happening just two years ago?

If I was writing *Open Life* today, I would have to consider the rise of enterprise distributions, in particular those of Red Hat and Novell, which are certainly worth covering in a book like this. On the other hand – at least, so I try to convince myself – it may still be too early to write anything definitive about them; especially Novell which is yet to finish reinventing itself, as is evident from the occasional eruptions of GNOME versus KDE discussions we witnessed last year. And in many ways it is version 10 of SUSE Linux Enterprise released just some weeks ago that is Novell's first serious stab at producing an enterprise distribution, so we will have to wait another year before assessing how well it has fared.

But in Part Two the content of one footnote struck me during proofreading of this edition. In it I mention a Microsoft project called Longhorn, which will produce the next version of Windows. In contrast to the whirlwind of development in Open Source and Open Content, the next version of Windows is still safely tucked into the development labs of Microsoft, and from what we hear it is not about to be released this year either. It serves as a soothing reminder, that not everything in our world moves as thrillingly fast, and is as hard to keep up with, as in the field of Open Source.

Now that Open Source has more or less established itself in the IT field, attention is increasingly turning to Creative Commons and similar Open Content projects, a development I very much predicted and hoped for in the first Finnish edition of this book. One interesting question right now is whether the collecting societies for musicians and other artists will ever allow their members to use Creative Commons licensing. In preparing for a lecture I was invited to give, I asked Teosto, the Finnish collecting society, what their official opinion was about that, and they told me: 'Of course we know about Creative Commons. The licences are OK for amateurs, but we will never allow our members to use them, that would be impossible.' To me, this sounds exactly the same as what IT people were saying about Open Source some ten years ago. So, now I always predict that ten years from now Creative Commons or a similar sharing system will prevail throughout the entertainment industry, and it will be interesting to see whether or not that prediction comes true.

I wish to thank Sara Torvalds and Helen Wire, respectively, for working on the translation and editing of this English edition. It has been an interesting year, and you both managed to grasp the style I was reaching for.

You were also fast to learn a great deal of specialized nerd-terminology, and soon started to hit the right words quite fluently, making me more and more a mere reader!

Finally, I also want to take this opportunity to thank all the readers of *Avoin Elämä: Näin toimii Open Source*, who throughout the last year have either sent me their feedback or written their responses to it in public places where Google would help me find them. There is nothing more rewarding than hearing the ideas and thoughts that have arisen as a result of someone reading my book. Many of you also asked whether there would be an English translation, since you had some non-Finnish-speaking friends with whom you wanted to share the book. I'm now so glad to say: Here it is!

henrik ingo
Espoo, 30 July 2006 (last day of my summer vacation)

Part One

in which thoughts fly high and Linux isn't even mentioned.
Or is it?

The French in crisis

Beaujolais in crisis. The secret is out!

That headline was in *The News*, an English-language newspaper published in France for foreigners and others interested in things French.[4] I had bought a copy to read on the train when I was backpacking across Western Europe. I had made it a habit to read not only the *International Herald Tribune* but a local paper in each country I passed through. However, having read physics rather than French in high school, I had to resort to a French newspaper written in English. And why not?

So, what was this crisis that the Beaujolais winegrowers were facing? Had frost or crows ruined the grape harvest? Or were killer grasshoppers on the loose?

Not even close. The crisis stemmed from 2001, an exceptionally good year for the Beaujolais harvest. Yes, it had been an *exceptionally good* year. But the following year complete disaster loomed, because the 2002 harvest was about to be *just as good*! For a while this information was kept quiet, a sordid fact known only to winegrowers and other wine-trade insiders. However, the secret was now out, and the poor winegrowers were facing ruin.

The law of supply and demand

We have all heard of the law of supply and demand. Even by reading *Asterix* one learned that the law of supply and demand is what sets market prices and seems to be what generally keeps the wheels of the economy turning.[5]

The law of supply and demand builds on mathematician Daniel Bernoulli's insight that the price of a product should not be determined so much by its production cost, but by how useful it is to its prospective buyer. If a buyer is willing to pay a lot for it, then a cheap product can be sold at a high price. According to a saying in Finland, it is not stupid to ask a high price, but it is to pay it.

Consequently, if the same product is available from more than one vendor, the buyer gains by taking his business to the one who offers it at the

---

4 'Beaujolais in crisis.' *The News, France's English Language Newspaper For Residents and Lovers of France.* No. 159/August 2002, p 1.

5 See *Obelix and co.*

best price. So, demand hikes up the price and supply brings it down, and somewhere along the line a balance is reached, and that is where business happens.

The law of supply and demand can lead to situations that seem strange when common sense is applied to them. OPEC is an organization whose members include most of the oil-producing countries of the world. The member countries decide between themselves how much oil each of them will produce in any given period. If brief reports in the news are to be believed, the Arab gentlemen of the organization essentially make one of two decisions: either to increase or decrease oil production.

And following one of the meetings in which they've decided to decrease oil production, you can bet that the news next day will announce the price of oil has gone up in the world. This is so normal, so mundane, it hardly raises an eyebrow. But let's think about it. The oil is no different to the oil that was on sale at a considerably cheaper price just the day before. It's no better or worse in quality, it's sold in barrels of the same size, it's exactly the same kind of oil, it's just more expensive. This is an example of the law of supply and demand in action. When supply goes down, the price goes up – even if all else remains equal.

Wine down the drain

Going back to the French winegrowers of Beaujolais, an unfortunate situation had occurred whereby supply exceeded demand. There was too much wine. If the secret were revealed, the prices might drop dramatically. And when the secret was revealed, there was a crisis.

But the French knew what to do. Professional wine tasters had already started dividing the wine into three categories. Only the best wine was to be sold. The middling wines would become vinegar, and the worst wines would be poured down the drain. The winegrowers knew the law of supply and demand and calculated that it made better business sense to sell less wine at a higher price than to sell more wine at a lower price.

Wineglass symphony

The smallest village shop, whether it is French or Finnish, follows the law of supply and demand, and to say that is hardly shocking news.

What is shocking, though, is that the law of supply and demand has sneaked outside its rightful territory into areas of which it should stay clear. For almost three centuries, we've been aware of the mechanism of supply and demand. It has become such an ingrained part of our thinking that its tentacles have reached even into areas of our lives that have nothing to do with commerce. When there is no connection to commerce, the result of the warped thought processes can be very sad. And the worst thing is, even as we implement it, when the law of supply and demand is operating outside the field of commerce, we don't necessarily recognize it as such.

When I first had Christmas dinner with my wife's family, it transpired that my father-in-law is the sort of person who always has a trick up his sleeve to entertain guests. In honour of the festivities, a table had been set with wineglasses – not however for us to drink Beaujolais from. As we were waiting for the dessert, my father-in-law wet his index finger and started showing us how to make music by running it around the rim of a wineglass.

Naturally, in such a situation, everybody starts trying to make their wineglass ring, and as I recall I was the last one to charm a reasonably pure note from my glass. So there we were, whining away together, when my father-in-law moved on to his grand finale: balancing a fork and a knife on the tip of a match over his wineglass. If you've never seen this trick performed at any of your festive dinners, please feel free to drop in sometime when we are visiting my in-laws in Jakobstad (Pietarsaari in Finnish). It's really worth seeing. But as it looked rather difficult, the rest of us didn't even try to do it. After the wineglass music and the match tricks, our Christmas lunch continued in high spirits.

Next, on New Year's Day, my wife threw a bachelorette party for a friend who had been her bridesmaid of honour, and for whom she was now matron of honour. The party included a dinner, during which – so I've been told – some drinking was done from wineglasses, and at some point my wife was inspired to show the others how to play them. As you have probably guessed, everybody at this party, too, tried their hand at ringing a tune from their glass.

Telling me about the evening afterwards, she was obviously a bit uncomfortable when she came to this part of it. When I asked her why, she finally confessed in a low voice that she rather regretted having shown all her friends how to play the glasses, because now everybody knew how to do it, it no longer seemed so special.

That was a sharp observation she'd made! A trick loses its value if everybody knows how to do it. There's no longer anything *special* about it. At least, this is how we always seem to think. On the other hand, you can't claim that music is more beautiful if you don't play it, than if you do. Or that an untold joke is funnier than a told one. And it can't be fancier to play a wineglass alone than to do it for an audience. But that is often how we think.

This story of playing on wineglasses is an excellent example of the notion of supply and demand on the loose outside the world of business. It slips into our everyday thinking and is so underhanded in the way it infects our *behaviour* that it goes unnoticed.

This way of thinking has been with most of us since we were children. It is what is at work when two children tell a third, 'We won't play with you!' It's as if their friendship grows stronger from *not playing* with others.

In addition to which, 'we' might 'have a secret that we're not telling you!' Children's secrets can seem amusingly insignificant to adults, but what a secret is about is not what matters – the important thing is that they are *not telling* it to others! Adults carry this exact same model of operations on into the world of trade secrets. Often, the kind of stuff branded a trade secret can also be absurdly insignificant, but the important thing is that they *don't tell others* about it. Today's companies are at least as interested in the things they don't do as the things they pretend to be doing and producing. And the doings of such companies aren't always any loftier than kids playing in a sandbox. In the Finnish magazine *Tietoviikko*, a columnist once wrote about his friend's experiences at a new media company that has since gone bankrupt. There, it was said, they generally spent more time writing non-disclosure agreements than they did doing any real business. In hindsight, the guy was quite happy about it. You really wouldn't want anybody to know about the kind of stuff that was going on inside the new media bubble!

In the light of these observations, there's an ominous sense that much of what we do is done with a *logic of mean-spiritedness*, whether it is in business or in our everyday lives! We handle our relationships with other people the same way Arabs handle oil production: 'After yesterday's meeting, OPEC announced that it won't play with you anymore.'

The morals of farming

The French Beaujolais article strengthened my stereotypical image of the French and particularly French farmers. They're immoral creeps, they *are*! And by that, I don't just mean that pouring good booze down the drain is immoral, even though a good number of my fellow countrymen would consider it so.

What particularly struck me about the article was that nowhere did it question whether or not there might be something even slightly irresponsible about pouring good wine down the drain – and this is me thinking of wine as a foodstuff now, not as an alcoholic beverage.

The job of a farmer is to produce food. Without food we die, so this is not an entirely unimportant issue under scrutiny here. And there's more to it than that, since you could argue that the point of working is to produce wellbeing – food, health, security, entertainment, and so on.

'Yeah, yeah,' I can hear you thinking, 'but wine is not food. The point of wine is to be rare and expensive, a treat. Otherwise there'd be no snob value! And snob value is half the fun of drinking wine. It's not as if they're pouring milk and potatoes down the drain.'

Maybe so. I've lost my faith in French farmers, but you might be right. Because nobody would actually throw away real food – would they?

They most certainly would, and do. I claim that, like everything else we're doing these days, the actions of farmers and governments are all too often based on a mean-spirited logic.

Mean-spiritedness and EU farming subsidies

As is widely known, all farming in Europe is based on a massive system of subsidies. For some reason it seems farming is such unprofitable work that farmers need to be subsidized if we are to have anything to eat.

I wonder if anybody knows all the political reasons behind the farming subsidies? The least likely of them might not seem to be national security.

But because we up here in the north have considerably less favourable weather for farming than our southern European friends, it really is a question of national security that our farmers get their subsidies. When it comes to the production of food, most people would consider it vitally important for each country to maintain a certain level of self-sufficiency. And because those of us living at Arctic latitudes can't possibly compete with the farmers in southern Europe, we must pay our farmers subsidies. Even I can see the point of that. What I don't understand is why French farmers also get subsidies, and in particular I don't understand why they get paid more than their colleagues in the north!

OK, so I don't understand the EU farming policy, that's OK. But I do know there's a lot of talk in the EU about *quotas*. There are quotas for milk, quotas for eggs, and quotas for grains. When a farmer gets a certain subsidy for his work, he also commits to *not exceed his quota*. Because, if farmers did exceed their quotas we'd have more food than the citizens of the EU could eat, and in no time we'd have the same crisis on our hands as the Beaujolais winegrowers.

In a word, Europe's farming policy is based on *mean-spiritedness*. The subsidies policy is based on farmers agreeing *not* to produce more food than their agreed quota. When one considers that a great number of people on Earth are starving and many of them actually die of hunger, this policy seems extremely questionable.[6] Yet this gets very little coverage in the media, perhaps because we've come to accept that being mean-spirited is normal and sensible. Ironically, both farming and commerce are often spoken of as being productive when actually it is being mean-spirited.

---

6 This does not deal with the fact that dumping European over-production in developing countries would also cause problems, as it would make their domestic farming unprofitable. However, this question also relates to the law of supply and demand.
   In the World Trade Organization negotiations on free trade held between the US, Europe, and several developing countries in 2003, a miracle occurred: pharmaceutical companies were willing to make concessions to their patents because the developing countries demanded it. In the end no deal was done because the countries in the EU, in particular, were not willing to give up their farming subsidies. For some reason that is just too hard for them.

Openness

The logic of mean-spiritedness that follows from the law of supply and demand, can also be found in all fields of commerce where there is any so-called 'immaterial property', including information technology (IT), music, film, and other kinds of entertainment, but the most glaring examples of it occur within the world of computers.

It is interesting that in the information business, handing over the *product* never means the giver has any less of it. Digital information can be endlessly copied. Einstein's famous dictum is true: 'If I give you a penny, you are a penny richer and I'm a penny poorer. But if I give you an idea, you have a new idea but I still have my own.'

Unfortunately, Einstein's principle has not been the guiding light in the IT business. Instead of treating digital information in the way most appropriate to it, it is treated as if it were a natural resource that is running dry. It is sold in cardboard boxes just as oil is sold in barrels.

An average computer program costs, let's say, a bit less than EUR 1,000. Of course there are more expensive software programs – large corporate systems can cost up to EUR 50,000 – but even a grand is a still lot of money. Usually, a computer program is bought in the tangible form of a CD, which is probably additionally packaged in a pretty cardboard box. The manufacturing costs for one CD, including the cover, is about EUR 1. The cardboard box is even cheaper. To that you'd have to add transport and warehousing costs, and the retailer must have their commission. But the fact remains: when we buy a computer program, 99 per cent of what we pay is for *nothing*.

Of course it's not really for nothing, because we're not buying just any CD, but one with some specific software on it. Computer programs obviously don't just self-generate, which means the programmers must also be paid. But even so, the physical mechanics of commerce in the field of IT is inappropriate to digital material. And that has given rise to a certain tension.

One way this tension is expressed is through *piracy*. Piracy means that a computer program (or any other product available through IT) is copied without permission of the originator. Copying, of course, doesn't cost anything, nor does it take anything away from anyone – that is in the sense that nobody has less computer programs than they had before some copying was done. However, piracy is illegal and a lot of time and money have been spent and tears shed in fighting piracy in both the IT and entertainment industries – almost as much as in the US versus Arabs fight over Iraqi oil.

But we also have a lot to learn, particularly from the IT industry, about breaking the cycle of mean-spirited business practices. An ever-increasing number of programmers are writing their software based on the principle of *Open Source*. In the Open Source movement, there is no ban on copying software. Actually, it's encouraged. There is no disguising of how the programs work; instead, the source code in Open Source programs is, as the name suggests, open and freely available.

The existence of Open Source programs in itself is hardly surprising. Thanks to the Internet, there need be no costs for distributing a program, which means it would be far more surprising if the Internet wasn't used to distribute free programs. What is extraordinary about Open Source is that in recent years it has become apparent that in many ways the Open Source programs are often better than the corresponding *closed source* programs. It would seem that by working in accord with the inherent nature of digital information, rather than doing its utmost to fight against it, the Open Source community has released an extraordinary resource, one hitherto much misunderstood and neglected within the IT industry.

The power of this is best illustrated by the question, if Open Source programs, such as Linux, are better or merely just as good as the corresponding non-open programs, then where do they come from? Who makes them, and who finances their work?

At first, it can look as if the Open Source programs are self-generating! Of course, that can't be true, and isn't. But when you ask who has made them, the answer is *nobody in particular*! For example, Linus Torvalds has been working on his Linux for more than a decade, but even so he has only written a small part of the code of the Linux kernel. Most of it has been written by somebody else. Who else? Many other like-minded people. Some do it for fun – Linus is one of them – others do it for work.[7] Aha, so what corporation are they working for? The answer to that is: several unconnected businesses. However you twist it and turn it, the end result is that no *one* person designed Linux, it wasn't financed by any particular

---

[7]   Actually, while this book was being written, Linus started working for a foundation called the Open Source Development Lab, where he is paid to work full time on Linux – for the first time in the twelve-year history of Linux. See also *Just for Fun: The Story of an Accidental Revolutionary* (2001), Linus Torvalds, David Diamond, Texere Publishing, US.

party, and you could almost begin to think it was self-generated! Behind Linux, there are lots and lots of programmers who are not mean-spirited!

The Open Source community is turning the practices of the IT industry upside-down. And what is most encouraging about this is that in practice Open Source code seems to be proving that mean-spiritedness is the worse option – openness is better. Could that also mean that music is more beautiful when played and that jokes are funnier when told? Can we learn to identify and eliminate the logic of mean-spiritedness wherever it's at work in other areas of life, so that along with open code, we can also have an open mind and live a more open and generous life?

Linux and Open Source

My aim here is not to prove Linux is better than Windows, or that Open Source is the only right solution. I'm certainly not trying to deny the fact that oil is a diminishing resource. But I do hope to prompt a bit of rethinking of some prevailing attitudes. Next, I'll be taking a look at the principles, values and practices of the Linux world and, who knows, we might even learn something from them.

Approaching the end of this introductory Part One it's probably a good idea to accept that some readers may never even have heard of Linux or the concept of Open Source. So, before proceeding any further, here's a short-and-sweet summary of the background to Open Source programming.

Average computer users believe, perhaps justifiably, that they have never used Linux. Most probably, they are using a Microsoft operating system called Windows together with other programs by Microsoft and a few other companies to handle their daily computing requirements. But indirectly all of us will have made use of programs produced by the Open Source community. The text you are reading right now has been written on a computer running on Linux, using a word-processing program called *OpenOffice*.

If you've used the Internet, you have definitely been in touch with a web server using the *Linux* operating system. More than 60 per cent of all website pages on the Internet are there thanks to an open server program called *Apache*. Most e-mails are passed on to their recipients through an open mail server program called *Sendmail*. These are all well-known Open

Source programs. So, quite unknowingly, you probably use Open Source programs on a daily basis!

As I explained earlier, the usual practice in a programming company is for the source code of a computer program, the text the programmer writes, the work itself, to be kept secret. Usually, it isn't shown to anyone outside the company, and the finished program is distributed only in machine code, that is in the form in which the computer uses it. In practice, it is impossible for anyone to read a program in machine code. In addition to which, the use of the program in machine code is limited through various legal clauses to which the buyer of the program must agree before the program will download onto their computer. One such typical clause states that the buyer agrees to install the program from one CD onto one computer only. So, if somebody has two computers they should buy two copies of the program they want to use, even though there is no technical reason for doing so.

The Open Source community work to a completely different set of principles when producing their programs. The use of an Open Source program is not artificially limited in any way. The source code is available to all and sundry. It can, for instance, be published on the Internet. Not only is the source code freely available for other programmers to read but also for them to use in their own programs, even though the code has been written by others.

In recent years, these simple principles have become a serious challenge to the traditional programming industry. Even though this industry is still going strong, it has begun to seem that systems based on Linux and other Open Source programs are often both cheaper and qualitatively better. Lately, many big information-system projects have been based on Linux. And as I have already said, for web servers, using Linux is the rule rather than the exception.

That's as far as this text will go in presenting the history or technical background of Open Source programs. However, for those who may want to read more I would recommend the following books and links.

Rebel Code: Inside Linux and the Open Source Revolution
Glyn Moody, Perseus Books Group, 2001
A narrative history of Linux and Open Source, with first-hand accounts from more than fifty interviews of prominent leaders in Open Source.

The Cathedral and the Bazaar

Eric S. Raymond

Available as a book: O'Reilly, 2001

On the Internet: http://catb.org/~esr/writings/cathedral-bazaar/

A seminal text of the Open Source movement, this essay presents the work culture and dynamics of the Open Source community. In the days when it was still necessary, this text played an important role in defending the financial viability of Open Source programs.

The GNU Project

Richard Stallman

Published in the book: Open Sources. O'Reilly, 1999.

On the Internet: http://www.gnu.org/gnu/thegnuproject.html

A look at the history of the Free Software movement by its founder.

The Open Source Definition

Bruce Perens

On the Internet: http://www.opensource.org/docs/definition.php

Ten principles that the licensing of an Open Source program must fulfil.

Just For Fun: The Story of an Accidental Revolutionary

Linus Torvalds and David Diamond. HarperCollins, 2001.

Autobiographical story of Linus Torvalds, which tells the history of Linux along with Linus' ideas on the meaning of life.

The Hacker Ethic

Pekka Himanen. Random House, 2001.

The Finnish philosopher's ethical take on the principles of the Open Source community.

Part Two

in which Linus is a dictator, laziness a virtue,
and hackers fight for their identity

Lessons learned in the world of Open Source

This book has no pretensions to being a history of Linux. Nor is it a technical guide to how Linux works. Moreover, as I am an engineer, I'll leave the writing about ethics to Himanen.[8]

In the world of software, the Open Source movement has successfully challenged traditional ways of thinking, which I have described in Part One as mean-spiritedness. But the software business is only one small part of the world, and I believe that other areas of business have a lot to learn from the Open Source movement. As private individuals, we all have something to learn from how these people have challenged the convention of mean-spirited business practices. Few of us may even notice that we now live in a world where we don't want to teach our friends how to play tunes on wineglasses. But even those of us who do notice may not have any alternative ways of functioning.

The aim of this book is to look at the culture of the Open Source community, its business and work ethics, and its values. The approach is very practical, and sometimes even resembles a case study. In this part of the book we will look at some of the principles and practices valued by the Open Source community, in the hope of learning something from them. Let's start with a subject which is bound to be useful for everybody: stress management *à la* Linus Torvalds.

The deadliness of deadlines

Linus Torvalds created the Linux operating system and is still in charge of Linux development. After graduating in computer sciences from the University of Helsinki in February 1997, he went to work for a California-based company called Transmeta. At the same time, Linux was becoming a relatively mature operating system, and was beginning to get attention from the press. When Linus moved to the United States it gave the American media far greater access to him, and thus the shy nerd was suddenly transformed into poster boy for the entire Open Source movement.

One of the most frequently asked questions at the time was, 'When will the next version of Linux be released?' Linus had a stock answer, which was always, 'When it's done.'

---

8   Pekka Himanen (1973), is a Finnish philosopher and perhaps best known for his book *The Hacker Ethic*, with Linus Torvalds and Manuel Castells. (See end of Part I.)

Long before Linus joined up, one of the mainstays of Open Source program development was that a program is released when it is ready. There are no deadlines, and the developers won't give even a rough estimate of any release date.

In his legendary essay 'The Cathedral and the Bazaar', Eric Raymond discusses this principle.[9] He comes to the conclusion that in a programming project, as in any project, there are typically three expectations: the finished product must have certain features; it must meet certain demands of quality; and it must be completed by a fixed deadline.

These three demands – features, quality, and deadline – would build a certain tension into any project. If, for instance, the schedule is too tight, there may not be enough time to include all the features you want. But if a project manager leans on his team, demanding that all the features are included *and* the deadline be met, then they are compelled to do a rushed job and, inevitably, quality suffers. Raymond concludes that by consciously abandoning just one of the demands, you can usually achieve good results on the other two.

In the light of that, the Open Source community's no-deadlines principle makes excellent sense, and is probably one of the reasons Open Source programs are so successful. This no-deadlines attitude is, of course, at odds with the project culture prevalent in the rest of the business world, where it is usual for there to be not just one final deadline but also several intermediate deadlines to be met at different stages along the way. Sometimes, to be such a project manager is to find yourself having to give greater priority to working out, following up, and constantly re-evaluating schedules, than to doing the actual work, thus the work itself becomes of secondary importance.

I experienced this firsthand not so long ago, when I was involved in a project for a large Finnish IT company.[10] At the first meeting, the client didn't even know in detail what the project was to be about. Making a precise list – defining the number of features – was to be part of the project. But the one thing that was clear right from the start was the schedule. Before we'd even defined what we were to do, we were given a deadline. And the 'well-justified' reason for it was that the project had to be realized within

---

9   http://catb.org/~esr/writings/cathedral-bazaar/

10   Unfortunately, I can't tell you the name of the company or about the project because, of course, the contract included a non-disclosure clause.

two months because its funding had to come from the budget for the current quarter. I don't know if this is an indication of the usual priorities within that company, but I certainly found it amusing.

However, my amusement lessened as the project deadline approached, and we made the finishing touches to the work late on a Sunday night. But the final project meeting was held within the specified time period, the invoice was sent on the last day of the quarter, and everybody was happy. Of course, this did require some self-deception, because we agreed to hold another meeting a few months later to sort out whatever had not been properly resolved by the time of the final meeting, and that turned out to be quite a lot. But that's fine – better to be a bit dishonest among yourselves than to compromise on quality. So, the project was pronounced a success and said to have been completed on time.

Quality and quantity of features are factors of the corporate world and of production. Perhaps some project manager will employ Eric Raymond's way of thinking in their next project. But more important is to understand the influence of deadlines on our own lives. To many people a deadline can seem like a matter of actual life or death, and they feel impelled to work like crazy late into the night to meet it. And very often this life-or-death deadline is totally arbitrary or – as in my own case – is fixed to comply with some utterly unproductive bureaucratic detail. And for *that* we allow ourselves to become so stressed?

Linus has tried to sort out his own approach to work in a principle he dubbed *Linus's Law*. It answers the question: why do people do things? The first reason is survival. The second reason is to have social life. And the third reason is that people do things for fun. In that order.

Linus's Law can be applied to work. Primarily, people work to earn enough money to buy food and pay to keep a roof over their heads. But if these were their only motivations, people could work a lot less than they do today. Somebody once said if it were only a question of getting the sustenance for survival, people in the Western world wouldn't need to work more than a few hours a week. By Monday afternoon, we'd have earned the essential part of our income. And in a welfare state like Finland, odds are one could survive one's entire lifetime without working at all.[11] But people still want to work. Why?

Work provides people with a social life. School and the workplace are where most of us get to know our best friends. So, that's the social-life motivation. And most people strive to get a job they think they will enjoy doing. So, they work for fun.

Since we work to have fun, to enjoy it, then why do we drive ourselves into the ground trying to meet artificial deadlines? Why work like drudges, as if it really is a question of life and death? Linus feels there's no sensible reason for it. You ought to enjoy work, because that's why you do it. Once again, it's clear that deadlines are bad for both the worker and the work itself.

Linux 2.2 was finally released on 25 January 1999. And almost immediately speculation was rife about when the next version, Linux 2.4, would be released.[12] By the time version 2.6 was released the press had learned to be patient, and nobody had bothered to ask Linus for a release date. The media had learned something. You, too, could try learning something from Linux. Take it easy and enjoy what you do.

Work undone

Another question Linus and other Open Source developers get asked a lot is, 'Why does your program not have this or that feature?' Those who ask such questions are not so often journalists as people who use a particular program, the clients so to speak. Naturally, the stock answer is, 'Because nobody's written it yet.'

That answer may seem a trifle brusque, particularly if it is then pointed out that, 'The program source code is freely available on the Internet. If you need a certain feature you are free to create it yourself.' Since it's quite likely the person who asked the question doesn't know the first thing about programming, that answer really can seem rather brusque.

However, there's a fair amount of healthy self-preservation in giving such an answer. Most Open Source programs are written by volunteers.

---

11 Naturally, everyone survives their entire life. :-) What I mean is that it's possible to live to become a pensioner without ever working a single day. Most people, however, don't want that sort of a life.

12 Linux versions are always denoted by even numbers. Odd numbers are development versions for programmers.

Linus Torvalds, for instance, began working on Linux while he was studying the programming of operating systems. It was his hobby, nothing more. When Linux became a version that worked to some extent, Linus kept developing it only for his own use, incorporating features which he found interesting. But whether Linus wanted it or not, Linux became popular. Others wanted to use his operating system. Getting a positive response to the work he had put in must have been flattering, but along with it came various requests, such as, 'There's this thing that doesn't work on my computer, could you fix it?' or 'It'd be really cool if Linux allowed you to ...' The inclination to please others is natural to human beings, especially when it relates to our life's work, we really want people to like what we're doing. But to be suddenly faced with thousands of requests can be overwhelming, and it's better to be a bit brusque than to drown.

Unfortunately, one also has to accept that there are a large number of people whose mission in life is to complain. For Linus, who was all excited about making a working operating system for himself, mixed in with the plaudits came the complaints, 'Linux doesn't have so and so,' and 'Linux can't do this or that.' Such people are never satisfied. And alongside them come the propeller heads wanting their ideas to be incorporated: 'I've been thinking you could add such and such a feature to Linux ...' But even if the feature they'd suggested was added to the program, they'd never use it, because by then they'd already have had ten other new ideas about what 'it would be so cool if you were to ...' The poor programmer would like to make all these Little Helpers happy, but if he tried, he'd find himself swamped by a never-ending stream of requests. What's worse is that too much popularity of this kind can be the death of a project that had got off to a good start.

With this in mind, a program developer's curt reply should be interpreted as a polite negative, a necessarily shortened version of, 'Because I work on this program as a hobby and for my own enjoyment, I unfortunately lack the time to realize the feature you suggest, and for which I myself have no need. However, I do think your idea is good and, if you want, you can realize it yourself because the code is freely available on the Internet. Working together is fun, too.'

In addition to self-preservation, there is another little seed of truth in the short answer. After all, if the person asking *really* needed the feature they'd mentioned, they could create it for themself or at least hire someone who could do it for them. Of course, many of these people are truly excited about their good ideas, but when put to them like this, they become considerably less excited. In reality, they don't believe enough in their great idea to invest more than a few seconds of their time chatting about it, or to invest a penny of their money.

A good friend of mine is a pastor, a job which I can tell you is far more varied than you might expect. In addition to performing religious services and wedding ceremonies, pastors have to provide all sorts of programs for young and old. Also, a pastor needs a working knowledge of sound systems, to be a computer support person, and to generate and get involved in all sorts of interesting projects. My friend has even delivered a live sermon on the Internet.

We once talked about how he plans his work. After the summer and winter vacations he usually writes a list of projects and whatever else needs to be done. If more good ideas crop up later, they can always be added to the list. He then chooses one or more projects and gets them started, and when each one is finished it is crossed off the list.

After six months, it's time for a new list. Happily, many of the projects on the old list will have been completed, but many of them will have remained undone. Like programmers, pastors seem to have more ideas than they have time. Undone projects are transferred to the new list.

Sometimes, a great idea can move from list to list for years, always stuck among the work that remains undone. In the end, such projects are struck from the list, and no more thought is given to them.

Unknowingly, my friend follows the same principle of prioritizing his work as do Linus and his colleagues. Like him, they list the features they'd like to realize in their programs – some they've come up with themselves, others have been requested by users. Then, everybody does what they feel like doing.

With everybody doing whatever they feel like, some things often stay undone for a long time, simply because they're things nobody feels like doing. This gives Linus no cause for concern. If some feature remains unrealized for years, it can't be all that important, as people have been getting along without it! What Linus teaches us here is that the important stuff will automatically get selected and done, so it need not be worried about.

Today, Linux is a billion-dollar business, with companies such as IBM and HP involved. If some feature is really needed, they can get it done themselves – and they do, because the code is freely available on the Internet.

Even if you don't happen to have a billion dollars, you can still apply this principle of the Open Source community in your own life. Next time your boss offers you a really important new project that must be done immediately, you can think: *If this project is really so important to the company, I'm sure they can hire somebody to do it who won't have to do it as overtime.*

Don't plan anything

The birth of Linux dates from the message that Linus posted to the Usenet system discussion group, comp.os.minix, on August 25, 1991. Of course there weren't any Linux discussion groups at the time.

```
From: Linus Benedict Torvalds
(torvalds@klaava.Helsinki.FI)
Subject: What would you like to see most in minix?
Newsgroups: comp.os.minix
Date: 1991-08-25 23:12:08 PST

Hello everybody out there using minix -

I'm doing a (free) operating system (just a hobby,
won't be big and professional like gnu) for
386(486) AT clones. This has been brewing since
april, and is starting to get ready. I'd like any
feedback on things people like/dislike in minix, as
my OS resembles it somewhat (same physical layout
of the file-system (due to practical reasons) among
other things).

I've currently ported bash(1.08) and gcc(1.40), and
things seem to work. This implies that I'll get
something practical within a few months, and I'd
like to know what features most people would want.
Any suggestions are welcome, but I won't promise
I'll implement them :-)

Linus (torvalds@kruuna.helsinki.fi)

PS. Yes - it's free of any minix code, and it has a
multi-threaded fs. It is NOT protable (uses 386
task switching etc), and it probably never will
```

```
support anything other than AT-harddisks, as that's
all I have :-(.13
```

There is a certain grandness in that quote, and you can practically hear the making of history. Looking back at this thirteen-year-old post, it is also rather endearing in its naivety. Today, Linux is big, and the work to develop it is done professionally. On top of which, it is probably the most portable operating system in history. At the time of writing, Linux supports the architecture of at least 16 different processors, from the IBM s390 mainframes to tiny processors used in consumer electronics. In fact, the Linux code is said to be exemplarily modular and therefore easy to port.

A further irony is that the GNU project mentioned by Linus still hasn't managed to finish its own 'big and professional' Hurd kernel. All credit to them for not having given up, though. I've been following the development of Linux closely for half a decade, and all that time Hurd has been almost complete. Somehow, it is amusing to see that their situation was much the same thirteen years ago, when Linux was born.

We often use the so-called great men of history as examples when trying to make some sense of our own lives. There is even a colourful set of professionals – psychologists, philosophers, dancers, hockey coaches, and who knows what else[14] – who make their living by talking about success at various business functions, and they too draw inspiration from many sources including history. Such people often talk about great visions, determination, and hard work.

Linus – undeniably a great man in the field of computer programming – is someone who doesn't fit the mould of these spirit-lifting talks. It seems that the guiding principles at work in the development of Linux have been the lack of vision and determination, or something we might prefer to call *openness*. Openness to other people's ideas. Openness to changes in plans.

I find it amusing to imagine what would have happened if Linus had been, say, 'determined'. When someone, in accordance with the principles of Open Source, first sent him the code to make Linux compatible with SCSI type hard disks, he might have answered, 'Thanks, but no thanks. After all, this is just my little unprofessional hobby and, as I wrote, I don't

---

13   The post can be read on the Internet at:
     http://groups.google.com/groups?selm=1991Aug25.205708.9541%40klaava.Helsinki.FI

14   These are the actual backgrounds of some popular Finnish lecturers.

36

have SCSI disks, so I won't be needing this code. And, anyway, I'm a bit busy right now, because I'm working really hard at the moment.'

Even if that is a ridiculous scenario, I'm sure there are stories just like it out there – stories of people who say 'thanks, but no thanks' to the chance of a lifetime. And possibly do so because someone giving a talk once advised them to be focused, determined and to work hard. But we don't often get to hear those stories, because those people rarely become the great men or women of history.

So, what is the secret of Linus Torvald's greatness? I think we can find in his story at least the following key principles:

- Linus does something he finds exciting.
- In addition to Linus being interested in operating system (OS) programming in its own right, Linux was from the beginning also a response to a tangible need: in 1991, the OSs for PCs were either lousy (dos) or expensive (unix) and that is why Linus decided to make an OS that corresponded better to his own needs.
- It could also be said that Linus was in the right place at the right time. He has said it himself: if he hadn't created Linux, somebody else would have.
- However, at the time Linus was the person who was open to the possibility when he encountered it, even though it wasn't what he had planned.
- Also, Linus didn't stay in his cubbyhole hiding his work, but shared it openly with his friends.
- One final important factor was that Linus didn't work alone. He was open to the ideas put forward by others, and open to collaboration. Furthermore, he based his work on that previously done by others (minix) and took advantage of tools created by others (bash, and gcc).

Of course, more bullet points could be added to the list, the kind of qualities inspiration consultants love. It is obvious that Linus Torvalds is among the most talented in his field. He has also worked hard with Linux, but it would be wrong to describe his input as 'hard work'. What he did was *excited work*, which is altogether different. So, it is not good to advise people to work hard, they need to do what excites them.

The lesson to be learned from this one of history's greats is: *Don't plan anything*, because you can't know what life will bring.

It would be unfair to end this section without a small tribute to the GNU project. Richard Stallman began the GNU project in 1984, and he is the person who first devoted his life to developing software in an open process. Even though the Hurd kernel was trumped by Linux, nearly all the basic tools used in the Linux OS came from the GNU project, including bash and gcc, which Linus mentioned in the post that marks the birth of Linux. So, even if we laugh a bit at the Hurd kernel (which Linus mentions only indirectly), it is only fair to say that a lot of the work behind what we now know as the Open Source movement was done by the GNU movement. Perhaps it is appropriate to end this section with the words of Richard Stallman. Here is his response to the argument that most of the Open Source software was born [only] to scratch a developer's personal itch: 'Maybe that happens sometimes, but many essential pieces of GNU software were developed in order to have a complete free operating system. They come from a vision and a plan, not from impulse.'[15]

Do whatever you like

Now that we've got off to such a good start with that inspiring analysis of Linux we've practically dealt with the subject matter of this section in the previous one. But that's fine, there's nothing wrong with being on the go.

An integral part of the ideology of the Open Source movement, which Pekka Himanen, for instance, has called *the hacker ethic*, is the rule: *Do whatever you like*.

So far, much of the Open Source programs has been written by volunteers. It works a bit like barn-raising or, to use the Finnish term, a *talkoot*. Despite the changing situation – with more and more companies and therefore paid employees getting involved – the volunteer tradition is still strong. It is usually as a direct consequence of using volunteers that the people involved are so, well, *involved*. Nobody is obliged to take part. Indeed, who would volunteer to do it if they were not interested? Their enthusiasm generates an atmosphere of huge excitement and inspiration. The high quality of Open Source programs is often attributed to this genuinely committed atmosphere. When you do something because you have to, from nine to five every day, the result is very different to how it is

15   http://www.gnu.org/gnu/thegnuproject.html

when a person does something they're truly excited by and really enjoy doing, and perhaps even feel is their life's work.

But the do-whatever-you-like principle is about more than the consequence of a barn-raising or volunteer attitude. At least, Linus Torvalds himself has gone deeper than that and found a way to express it. In addition to the growing media interest in Linux in the late nineties, there was also a growing interest among programmers. Along with working hackers, many computer science students wanted to get to know Linux and to get involved in its development. For some, this offered an interesting challenge, while others probably only got involved because it was considered cool.

One consequence of this fashion fad was that people started contacting Linus because they wanted to get involved in developing Linux. When they sought his advice about what they should start doing, he came up with another curt answer: *Figure out what you're interested in, then join in by doing that.*

Linus knew why he gave such non-specific answers. If he arbitrarily suggested that people get involved with this or that project, possibly something currently fascinating to himself, his advice was bound to prove inappropriate for the other person. For one thing, the person seeking advice would probably not be interested in the same things as Linus, and would have a different range of abilities. So, anyone who was given specific advice would probably soon get frustrated with the whole project and end up being angry with both Linus and Linux. Also, no project can benefit greatly from a volunteer who isn't really keen on their part of the work.

Once again, such an attitude presents a real challenge for the corporate world. It's a challenge for Linux, too, now that the corporate world itself is getting involved in the development of the operating system (OS). How many employees can choose to do exactly what they want to do at work? And how many employees must do what the boss tells them to do? Is it even possible to implement such a *do-whatever-you-like* principle in the corporate world?

If we accept that the *do-whatever-you-like* principle is a cornerstone of the Open Source community, it follows that we might expect that the same principle applied in the corporate world would generate the kind of success it has for Linux.

Usually, the vision and business strategies which guide a company are created in the upper echelons of management, after which it's up to the employees to do whatever the boss requires of them. How strictly this tradition is imposed varies from company to company but most employees accept that it is the way things are and, indeed, the way they should be. But the principle of *do whatever you like* would suggest that management – in accordance with the principle of *don't plan anything* – should quit producing the whole vision and business strategies, and focus instead on making it possible for employees to realize their own vision as best they can. For many managers such a concept would seem totally alien.

Those of us who are not corporate big-shots are always faced with the question, 'Am I doing what I really want right now?' When you chose your present place of work, did you go for the job offering the highest salary or the one you were most interested in? This question is not only relevant for the sake of your own mental health, but should also be of interest to your employer. When enthusiasm for the work is so much better in the Linux universe, why should the corporate world settle for employees who merely put in their hours from nine to five?

So, do Linus Torvalds and the other hackers follow their own advice? Yes, they do. Today, all the foremost Linux programmers work for companies where their main job is Linux programming. Their hobby and their life's work has become their day job as well. Could you imagine a better existence? Never settle for less!

Laziness is a virtue

You may be surprised to hear that the first and foremost virtue of a programmer is laziness. In the Linux community laziness is acknowledged and valued above even eagerness and interest. Well, if you happen to be married to a hacker, you may already know they're a lazy bunch; there's never any help with the washing-up, not a chance of a hand with the laundry – in fact, often, a hacker even forgets to eat. However, others may find it hard to understand how Linus, for instance, can be said to be lazy; he is, after all, the kid who more or less locked himself in his room for a year, sitting up at all hours writing the code for the first Linux version.

The logic of the claim goes like this: the lazier the programmer, the more code he writes. When a programmer hits a boring, time-consuming and high-on-routines task, he gets lazy. There is nothing worse for a lazy hacker than boring routine tasks. That's why he decides to write a program that will do the routine tasks for him. This is the program he sits up all night to perfect, seemingly diligently at work. Typing is too arduous for him, so he writes the code for a word processing program. And because it's too much effort to print out a letter and take it to the postbox, not to mention licking a stamp, he writes the code for e-mail. Now you'll understand how truly lazy programmers are.

So, laziness is a programmer's prime virtue. It's good to remember this contradictory and somewhat amusing claim, because it's all too easy to forget why computers and computer programs – along with all other technology – were originally invented.

A new nuclear power plant is currently being built in Finland. Before the decision was made to build it, there was lively debate for and against nuclear power. One Member of Parliament who debated the question suggested that more nuclear power would be bad for Finland because the other ways of producing energy employed more people. Now, I must emphasize that I think there are many good reasons *not* to build more nuclear power plants in the world, but this was the most ridiculous argument I've ever heard, and I retain the right to laugh in the face of such an absurd argument.[16]

Naturally, you could actually produce electricity by having all the unemployed people in Finland pedal exercise bikes hooked up to dynamos, which in turn would be hooked into the power grid. That would probably give enough energy to light a fair-sized village, not to mention the added benefit of guaranteeing employment for everybody. But you'd be crazy to do it that way.

Surely, the point of having electricity is to free people from having to work so hard. We've come up with machines that run on electricity and do the job for us while we lie on the sofa watching television, which also runs on electricity. Lots of politicians seem to forget this, particularly when they talk about unemployment.

Don't misunderstand me. Losing a job can be one of the greatest misfortunes to befall us in life. Many people would rather be both ill and divorced, as long as they could keep their job. And some unemployment almost always follows technological advances. When the tractor was invented, farmhands lost their jobs and people moved to the cities. Luckily,

---

16 Tee hee hee. Woah woah woah.

they found manufacturing factories there, and got themselves jobs working on conveyor-belt production lines. But today, when a factory updates its production lines, one result of installing more advanced production machinery is that it inevitably requires less people to run it. And, once again, working people are made redundant.

But don't blame the engineers. Thanks to engineers, we no longer have to ruin our backs ploughing the soil. Thanks to engineers, machines now do the heavy work in factories with people overseeing it. Thanks to engineers, most of us have more free time to use in any way we choose, which is what we wanted when they were still inventing the tractor. The point of inventing and developing machines, computer software, and suchlike is that we won't need to work – or at least not work so much.

It's an unfortunate conundrum of modern society that the work that *is* available is unequally divided so that some people work as hard as ever in the factories, while others are left entirely without work. Perhaps here, too, we should learn from the Open Source way of thinking and employ the principles of openness and sharing. Perhaps the engineer who invented that first tractor actually meant for everybody to have some work to do – enough, but not too much – and for us all to enjoy our fair share of idle moments too.

Benevolent dictator

We'll leave the values of Linus and his friends for a while and turn to learning something from the organization and hierarchies of the Open Source community. How do you control a programming project that involves tens – or, in the case of Linux, hundreds – of programmers working in different parts of the globe, particularly when the workers are volunteers who have no official status as employees on the project?

Linus is the *benevolent dictator* of the Linux project. He didn't coin the expression himself; it comes from Eric Raymond's essay 'The Cathedral and the Bazaar', in which the author studies the various organizational forms of Open Source projects. Although the dictatorship model is not the only way Open Source projects are run, it is by far the most common and the least formal. Guido van Rossum, the creator of the programming language Python, is known publicly in Python circles as BDFL – Benevolent Dictator for Life. Apparently Python programmers have no intention of ever letting poor Guido enjoy a well-earned retirement.

A benevolent dictator is the leader of a project and the person who alone has all the power to make decisions.[17] Often this authority is a natural consequence of the leader being the instigator of the project, as Linus is in the case of Linux.

For those of us living in Western democracies, talk of dictatorship could sound suspicious. Although the directness of a dictatorship is sure to be cost-effective and helps to create a light organizational structure, history has taught us something about the problems inherent in such a system. Alas, few monarchs or dictators have ever been known for their benevolence. So, despite the cost, inefficiency and frustration caused by the negotiations, compromises and voting in a democracy, we have learnt the lessons of history and chosen to live under a democratic system of government. Linus Torvalds may score well above average for benevolence, but can we really trust that his successor – when that day comes – isn't a total disaster?

The answer is *yes*, because it isn't as if Linus is the leader of Linux by chance and it's just a lucky fluke that he is benevolent. Actually, it's quite the other way around: he's the leader only – and I repeat – *only* because he's as smart as he is.

The principles of Open Source generate a curious dynamic, which directly influences the hierarchy of the project organization and the relationships of its members. What would happen if for some reason Linus decided to screw things up and out of spite started making stupid decisions for Linux? Within twenty-four hours the other Linux developers would leave him to fool around on his own, make a copy of the Linux source code somewhere Linus couldn't get his hands on it and keep working without him. It's also extremely likely that the hackers involved would quickly elect – more or less consciously and more or less democratically – a new benevolent dictator.

All that is possible because the code itself is open and freely available for anyone to use. As dictator, Linus has all the authority while at the same time having no power whatsoever. The others see him as their leader only because he is so talented – or benevolent. There is a fascinating equilibrium

---

17   At this point, I'm sure, all the project managers reading this woke up and started to pay
      serious attention!

of power and freedom. The dictator has the power and the others have the freedom to vote with their feet.

But in some other environments the dictator model doesn't work so well. If your boss isn't up to his job, it's a bad thing, but what can you do about it? The army must blindly obey its commander-in-chief, but if he proves to be a sick tyrant what choice do the soldiers have about what they do? Such situations lack the openness that is inseparable from the Open Source process. Without openness there can't be complete trust in other members of the organization; instead, we are stuck with having to use the unwieldy processes of democracy to protect ourselves against power struggles and a variety of other forms of mean-spiritedness. Openness is so integral to the system of an Open Source project that such precautionary measures aren't necessary.

As a dictator Linus Torvalds is living evidence of the benefits of the openness principle. Openness leads directly to Open Source projects being free of the usual excess of inhibiting project organization, and to them getting along in a way that is surprisingly lightweight, nimble and cost-effective. Could that mean the dictatorship model might work in a more traditional organization? There is at least one example of it being so.

The World Wide Web Consortium (W3C) is a standardizing organ that has created nearly all the technologies that constitute the World Wide Web. Standards published by the W3C are, among others, HTML, CSS Style Sheets, XML, DOM (part of JavaScript), the PNG and SVG image formats and lots of other technologies of which we make daily use by surfing the Web. Some 450 IT businesses and organizations are members of the W3C, beginning with Microsoft and IBM.

Interestingly, the decision-making process of the W3C as it prepares standards resembles that of the Open Source dictatorship model. Preparation of a standard is done in a working group specialized in the field, and it works very openly. Trial versions of the standards are released so that anybody can comment on them. When the working group is ready, the proposal is brought to a vote. All member organizations are eligible to vote and each of them has one vote.

After the vote the W3C leader alone either approves or discards the proposal, no matter what the result of the vote. In practice, the W3C strives to get everybody in agreement, but the decision-making system itself clearly resembles the benevolent dictator model.

Since the W3C was founded, Tim Berners-Lee has been its leader. He is the same guy who developed HTML and other Web technologies while working at CERN in the early nineties. He is the Linus Torvalds of the Web – creator and dictator.

As at the W3C, decisions regarding the development of Linux are usually made after thorough discussion. Linus in particular takes the advice of his closest and longer-term colleagues, who within the community are known as his lieutenants. These lieutenants are like mini-dictators, and each one has their own area of responsibility within the project. Just as for Linus, their authority is based on talent proven over a period of years and the trust that it has generated. The dictatorship is therefore a *meritocracy*.

There have also been instances where, despite Linus being against a particular solution, he has grudgingly had to accept what is wanted by the majority. If he didn't, one day he might not be the dictator anymore. The open system works lightly, but is nonetheless democratic.

Tolerance

Having acquainted ourselves with some of the interesting features so characteristic of the Open Source community we will now consider other aspects of it. It must be said that tolerance is *not* a characteristic of this fascinating community, nor a prerogative of it. If you look at various discussion groups and mailing lists, it's easy enough to find numerous examples of Open Source community members who are anything but tolerant. Despite this, there are plenty of inspirational tales of tolerance that can be told about this community.

Once again, let's go back to Linus Torvalds and the years when the IT press discovered the fascinating and fresh operating system called Linux. This was at a time when Microsoft had managed to create a monopoly in both operating systems and office programs and was putting all its weight behind finally crushing Netscape, its rival in the browser market. This was a time when users had good reason to groan about the lack of alternatives, and were annoyed by the Microsoft monopoly and the abuses it entailed, and also by the flaws and surprising quirks of Microsoft programs, including the animations of squirming paper clips. In computer circles, people were actually beginning to see Microsoft as the root of all evil, hence the term the

Evil Empire. Naturally, being the new kid on the block, Linux was of great interest to IT journalists, particularly considering whether David had come to slay Goliath? Would Linux dethrone Microsoft?

Once more, Linus Torvalds had a surprising but wise answer. He stated that Microsoft and its programs were of no particular interest to him, since he didn't use Windows himself. He had worked on Linux for his own amusement, not because he had an axe to grind with Microsoft or anybody else.

Although many of Microsoft's competitors, then and even more so today, see Linux precisely as the OS to challenge the Microsoft hegemony, it is important to understand that for Linux developers that is not a primary consideration. For the most part, they really don't have an opinion about the whole world of Windows, because they use Linux.

Having used Microsoft software myself, I completely understand the journalists' view, but it is nonetheless hard to imagine that Linux would have been such a success if its main *raison d'être* had been merely to replace Windows. Programmers involved in such a mean-spirited project are unlikely to have been as innovative as those working on Linux, who put in their hours out of love for OS programming. From the outset, such a project would have been doomed to become no more than a Microsoft-aping dog with more bark than bite. Sure, perhaps it could challenge Microsoft products in some areas, but in others it would be just as lame and unimaginative as that which it was intended to outdo.

More than anything, however, Linus Torvalds' tolerant attitude makes sense for the sake of his own mental health. It's not healthy for one's central motivation to be hatred and fear. And, what if one day Linux did manage to bring down Microsoft? Would life then lose its meaning? In order to energize themselves, would the programmers then have to find some new and fearful threat to compete against?

People whose actions stem from this idea of having to outdo some perceived threat usually end up in just such a vicious circle. Take the US Army, for instance. You'd have thought that the fall of the Soviet Union would have been a happy day for American soldiers and CIA spies. It was no such thing. Far from it! All it meant to them was looming unemployment. They therefore needed to conjure up a new threat somewhere and find it fast. First they tried painting dark clouds in the shape of international drug dealing. For some reason that didn't quite have the cachet of an enemy nuclear state, so they had to look elsewhere. Now they've finally got their ideal enemy. Terrorists. They are apparently everywhere, but can't be found. That means there's plenty of work to be done in defending the nation, the money keeps coming in, and motivation is high. Again, the United States of America is a force to be reckoned with.

Although it's even more fun to pick on US foreign policy than on French farmers, we need to remember that more than anything we are now talking about ourselves and what motivates us. Lots of people build their lives on just such threat-based thinking and manage to create great drama out of this or that. It is the source of their vitality. Yet, if they chose to, they could be living happy and satisfying lives working on their own *Linux,* without wasting their energy on the artificial drama with which they surround everything.

To me, Linus Torvalds' example of tolerance shows great insight. As a talented programmer he cannot accept programs with bugs on his own computer, but their existence as such does not bother him. He can do a better job of writing code himself and is happy with the work he does. At the same time, it wouldn't bother him at all if everybody else wanted to use Windows instead of Linux. After all, that's not his problem. In a world of power struggles and perceived threats, Linus's tolerant attitude is breath of fresh air and an *open source* of peace of mind for everyone.

Diversity

In the summer of 2003, someone wrote to the Open Source website Advogato to say he thought the market of Open Source software was too splintered and confusing. Counting only the text editors, it included over 100. Being someone who had just switched to Linux, this made him feel lost. It would have been easier, if people could have agreed on which editor to use, developed it to its peak, and taught everyone how to use it.

This suggestion wasn't particularly well received. Most responses to it just said that the writer must not yet be very well acquainted with Open Source. The 100 editors are a sign of the wealth in the Open Source world. Naturally, it is true that most of them may be somehow deficient and were born as an assignment for some computer science student. But why is that a problem? It's great that he too published his work for open use, even though I don't happen to use that particular editor.

And also, as simple a thing as editing clean text files may actually require very different tools. For instance, the *vi* editor was created in the seventies and must be one of the simplest and most clumsy tools ever seen in the computing world. Despite this, or actually precisely because of it, it is part of the Unix standard and will be found in all the Unix machines in the world, including all Linux computers. So, if you learn to use *vi*, you can rely on getting the job done. It works on all platforms, regardless of whether you use it over a remote connection on a 'terminal' or in the graphical user interface (GUI) of a standard desktop PC. But in the latter case, you may want to use a more versatile editing tool, designed for a GUI environment. So you choose one of those. In fact, many of us choose the software we use based on personal likes and dislikes – such as colour. So, although it is an appealing idea to get rid of overlapping work by developing only one text editor, or a couple of editors at most, the problem would soon arise of how to choose which one should have the honour. Who gets to judge what taste other users should have?

This kind of splintering is also evident in another area. That is, the Linux universe currently has two windowing environments: KDE and GNOME.[18] This occasionally gives rise to concern among Linux users. Even though the programs made for GNOME work in KDE and vice versa, they may look different and follow slightly different principles. In all fairness, this can seem very confusing for a novice. One could also ask whether it makes efficient use of the available resources. Could there be a better way of employing programmers than by spreading their effort over two competing projects?

However, despite all the problems I've mentioned, the Open Source community is unanimous in feeling that the diversity available in Linux – even though it is sometimes inefficient – is valuable. We must always return to the guiding principles of Open Source, as discussed earlier in this book. Programmers do whatever they like to do – what excites them. If someone wants to make GNOME software, who's to stop them? And who loses if someone makes GNOME programs, even when everyone else wants to use KDE programs? These principles inevitably lead to diversity, because the

---

18   A windowing environment is the part of a computer program that creates a so-called *graphical user interface* on the screen. Other programs are used within this environment, and are activated by pointing at them with one's mouse, etc. Its opposite is a *terminal* or *command line interface*, usually operated via a keyboard, where the letters on the screen are a light colour against a dark background, and only one program at a time is used.

Open Source community is not Soviet Russia, where everybody must follow whatever five-year plan is currently in force.

There are also benefits to be gained when different projects compete with one another. The making of graphical user interfaces is a relatively young science, and nobody really knows which is the one and only right way of getting things done.[19] Competing projects may come up with different solutions to the same problem, and not until later does it become clear which of them provided the wiser and smoother solution. Thus, the existence of two separate projects lessens the risk of the GUI world of Linux ending up in a technological cul-de-sac.

Competing projects are also genuinely useful to each other. Even though from the outset KDE has been more technically advanced, GNOME was originally considered a very artistic environment. By using different themes users could make their own environment look very different to that of their neighbours, in effect customizing the look of their computer to suit their own individual taste. Surprisingly, many people particularly like to have this feature in their computer. What wallpaper you use and the colour of your program can sometimes seem a lot more important than what is actually done on the computer. So, the KDE programmers have put a lot of effort into developing these features in their own project and today KDE is at least as colourful and artistic as GNOME. Similarly, in order to catch up with KDE, the GNOME developers have worked hard to improve the stability and technical qualities of their environment.

So, competition obviously benefits both parties. Luckily, the developers of KDE and GNOME understand this. Even though there's a lot of debate on the Internet about the various merits of KDE versus GNOME – and sometimes, in the spirit of the Advogato writer, someone suggests that one of the projects ought to be shut down in the name of simplicity – the people who engage in such debates are never the programmers involved in developing either KDE or GNOME. Firstly, they don't have the time to engage in futile Web debates, because they have better things to do. But

---

19 Even though Apple and Microsoft have made graphical user interfaces for more than a decade, this is a relatively short time and theirs are only two views on how to do it. Even the Windows user interface has developed and keeps developing – XP has recently moved to a new look and Microsoft has announced that it works with a project called *Longhorn*, which again will lead to new technologies and practices. In addition, the X windowing architecture used in a Unix-type OS that is different to that of Windows or Apple, so the Unix world cannot take everything from Windows, but in any case the developers of KDE and GNOME have to do a lot of genuine pioneering work.

more essentially, they don't see each other as rivals. Instead, they recognize competition as a form of collaboration, despite the rest of the world not always seeing it that way.

This leads us to a final question. How does the rest of the world view it?

Even though by definition the Western market economy requires free competition, in reality companies don't always see it as a good thing because competition tends to mean less money in their particular till. Therefore, it seems the smart thing to do is to get rid of the competition, by whatever means. Microsoft is a prime example of how financially rewarding this strategy can be – when it works, it is very lucrative. This leads to Western companies – who one would expect to believe in a free market economy, and who probably genuinely *think they believe* in that – in practice, doing all they can to prevent competition. If one believes in the validity of the Open Source way of working, then companies that try to crush competition are actually digging their own graves.

Courage and curiosity

The installation guide to the popular Linux distribution Debian Linux includes a slightly scary term borrowed from electrical engineering to refer to the first time you start the computer after installing the operating system. It calls this first test run a *smoke test*. Originally, electrical engineers used the term *smoke test* in their building projects. For instance, after soldering components to a circuit board, they must then hook it up to the current. If the work has been done correctly, the circuit board operates as intended. If, on the other hand, there's a short circuit somewhere, the typical response would be for the soldered components to pop off the board and produce a wisp of smoke – a sure sign that the circuit board wasn't working.

Being immaterial, a computer program can't produce smoke, of course, but just the same the first time you start a computer with a newly installed operating system is always a moment of truth. It either works or it doesn't. The only way to find out is to try it.

Much like engineers, Linux programmers are driven by a burning sense of curiosity. For instance, they really want to know what new and fancy features Linus Torvalds' latest version of the Linux kernel will have, even before the kernel is complete. These unfinished Linux versions are called development versions, because they haven't yet reached the release stage. Although it's not recommended that you use them, they are just as available on the Internet as the officially released versions, and many a curious Linux user does come to use them before the final release.

Acting on this curiosity takes a kind of foolhardy courage, as there's always a risk in using an unstable development version of a new computer program. It may not work. And, particularly when the newly installed program is an entire operating system, there's always the risk that a malfunctioning program will tie your computer up in knots – such serious knots that you may lose all the data you had on your computer. Nonetheless, curiosity often wins out, and the eager user will disregard all risk and dull cautionary measures and give in to the irresistible temptation to try it out.

I was once given a laptop to work on but its battery was failing. I wanted to know if the battery was completely dead, or whether it was of the common sort that can keep a computer up and running for about five minutes before it finally conks out. Naturally, there are many ways to establish this, including, for example, sending the battery away to be serviced or borrowing a multimeter from an electrical engineer ... or use another method which is by far the quickest and therefore the best way for me to satisfy my curiosity.

So, I pulled the plug on my laptop. It died instantly. Which was unfortunate because I'd forgotten to save the text I'd been writing. However, despite this setback, my curiosity had won and the test had told me immediately what I'd wanted to know: the battery was 100 per cent out of order.

It may seem odd to describe Linux developers as courageous. The stereotypical image we have of an average computer programmer is of someone who is very likely to be shy, cautious and quiet, a person of perpetual bad-hair days, wearing unfashionable glasses – a nerd. I'm not suggesting all programmers fit the stereotype, but Linux programmers are often as close as you can get to a real-life version of it. That's why it's so surprising that such a bunch of nerds could be considered brave, but the anecdote above does indicate that nerds, despite their tendency to be shy and cautious, are courageous when it comes to computers. Their curiosity about computers overcomes all caution and can transform the shyest nerd into a courageous pioneer.

So far, this book has portrayed the Linux community as an admirable model for us readers, but this section on courage might be where the shy nerds at the heart of that community have the most to learn from themselves.

Let's imagine, for instance, what would happen if a shy and cautious nerd is sitting alone at a table in the lunchroom at his college or place of work, when a beautiful woman he doesn't know sits down opposite him. The most likely scenario is that absolutely *nothing* would happen! The nerd would stare at his food, eat it in silence, and leave. If the beauty on the other side of the table also happens to be a timid and quiet nerd, she is likely to do the same. Nothing can happen even by accident, despite the fact that these two people could find one another of interest.

What is the train of thought going through the nerd's head that leads to nothing happening? He'd certainly be interested in establishing contact with the beauty opposite, so surely he ought to speak to her. But nothing sensible comes to mind, and therefore no contact is made. Obviously, he should say something, anything, but then the nerd fears the beauty might think him stupid. And besides, such a beautiful woman would surely have been snapped up already, and even if she hadn't it's highly unlikely she'd be interested in *him*. The nerd daren't risk being turned down. He fears if he said something the answer, or rejection, might be chillingly polite. The nerd really doesn't want to risk that. So in the end the nerd says *nothing*, and that's what happens.

If the beauty were a computer, the nerd would behave differently – courageously. With the beauty sitting opposite there would come a moment of truth – time for a *smoke test*! The nerd would say something, despite the high likelihood of getting a chilling puff of smoke in the face. It's not as if this nerd hasn't had his share of failed smoke tests with computer programs, and they have never slowed him down. Actually, the nerd doesn't even see such failures as failures. They are just different experiments and just as much fun and educational as the successful tests. And it's only through failed smoke tests that you finally get to the ones that don't fail.

Had the nerd applied this same logic to approaching the woman, he'd have spoken to her right from the start. Her reaction would either have been positive or negative. But as far as the nerd is concerned, both reactions are useful and productive, because they immediately satisfy his curiosity and desire to try new things. Not even a rebuff means failure for the nerd; it's just a smoke test and whatever the result you are then free to go on and try something else.

Names and identity

Interestingly, the Open Source community which swears by openness and sharing does hold on to one thing, its names. And they do so to such an extent that this community, which has turned ownership and copyright practices upside-down, sees trademarks – which equals legal protection of a name – as a relatively positive thing. *Linux*, for instance is a trademark registered to Linus Torvalds, which means you can't call just any old operating system or some other software Linux. Linus allows only operating systems built on the Linux kernel released by him, and later modifications thereof, to be called Linux.

Respect for the name of a person or project is also one of the defence mechanisms of openness. The term Open Source itself is protected, and you can only use the term 'OSI certified Open Source' about programs that meet certain criteria of openness.

In the Open Source community, everybody is openly what they are – themselves. In releasing new versions of Linux, Linus Torvalds uses his own name. You can trust that a program called Linux is actually a program by Linus, and not something else. The name Linux guarantees the quality. The person who has worked to create a certain product personally guarantees its quality. And at the same time the work gives him or her credit. The programmer usually becomes famous as a result of their program. Even though people are happy to share the fruits of their labour, the kudos is not shared. And how could you, that wouldn't even be honest. Honour where honour is due: the person who did the job should get the credit. In a community, where everything is open and shared, this is something to hold on to. You've got to be able to trust some things.

But the Open Source community's relationship with names is a lot stronger than mere questions of trademarks or branding. Some words are closely connected to the identity of the community, and these people are willing to fight for them, even when the rest of the world may not quite understand what the fuss is about.

One of these identity-charged words is *hacker*. Most readers of this book will probably understand *hacker* as synonymous with *computer criminal*. To them, a hacker is a person who breaks into somebody else's computer system through the Internet, reads confidential files and perhaps also wreaks havoc in the invaded computer system. Even IT journalists erroneously use the word in this sense.

In the Open Source community, however, the word *hacker* has a very different meaning. In the early days of computers, in the nineteen-sixties and seventies, programmers at MIT and other American universities called themselves *hackers*. As the Unix OS (operating system) evolved, the word spread to the community surrounding it. Unix programmers were known as *hackers* or *Unix hackers* and they were still mostly university people. The word had no criminal connotation, rather it purveyed the notion of a very talented programmer, a guru and member of the Unix community, of someone who was passionate about programming and technology.

The ideology of the early hacker culture was very similar to the present-day Open Source culture. Not that there was such a concept as *Open Source*; it was more that all computer programs were open. For a culture that had been born in university circles, this was perfectly natural. The transition to the closed software culture we came to accept as normal didn't come about until the eighties, and it also caused the hacker culture to get a bit side-tracked. The mean-spiritedness that led to the manufacture and sales of closed software was in no way part of hacker culture.

At some point the press started reporting on information break-ins and for some reason began to call the perpetrators *hackers*. To begin with, it may not have been such a bad name to use because, unlike now, in those days anyone able to break into a computer system had to possess a lot of skill and talent, so in that sense they may well have been a genuine hacker. But from then on, the word *hacker* came to denote a computer criminal.

I've often wondered why the members of the Open Source community are so stubborn about still calling themselves hackers? The original meaning of the word has been so completely overshadowed by the new definition that it seems downright odd for any law-abiding citizen to still *want* to be referred to by that name. Even people working in the computer business are often confused, because the original meaning of the word *hacker* is not well-known outside genuine hacker circles. One ill-informed journalist even managed to write a long article about the notorious computer criminals who had created a new operating system called Linux! Apparently, nobody had ever told him that the meaning of the word *hacker* had become corrupted. Reading his article, I didn't know whether to laugh or cry.

But I do understand the hackers. How could anyone give up the name that defines their identity? The name that carries such a long and honourable history, harking back to the first computers and artificial intelligence laboratories.[20] The name that epitomizes the ideological foundations of the whole community, the foundations that Richard Stallman says so much about and that the philosopher Himanen so loftily proclaims in his book *The Hacker Ethic*. Despite all the confusion, hackers are proud to be hackers. And I have to admit I understand that with all my heart. It's not as if we Finns would change the name of our country just because the word *finni* or *finne* means a zit in a number of other languages![21]

There is another story to do with words which engages hackers as strongly as does the word *hacker*. But this time it's about words that don't unite hackers but rather cause strife among them.

When commercial closed software took over more and more from the hacker culture within universities, one man decided to make it his life's work to fight the mean-spiritedness of the corporate approach. In 1984 Richard Stallman announced that he had founded the GNU project. The aim of the project was to produce free software – or rather, *Free Software* – and one day release a completely free operating system.[22] Richard Stallman was not your average propeller-head. He really was 100 per cent committed to his project. He resigned from his job as a university researcher to ensure that the university could have no claim of ownership on the programs he made, which they could do if he had developed them while employed by them. Stallman's boss at MIT was himself something of a visionary. When he realized why Stallman was resigning, he ordered that Stallman's former office and other university services – particularly the computers – would

---

20 That's another funny name. Even though computers have developed amazingly since those days, true artificial intelligence has yet to be invented. To us today, computers of the sixties were nothing but electricity-hogging heat resistors whose calculating power couldn't compete with that of the simplest pocket calculator. Even so, the term *artificial intelligence* was bandied about at the time.

21 Next time you talk about computer criminals, it would please the hackers if you used the term they use: *crackers*. I, at least, would like to reserve the word *hacker* for those people of high principles about whom this book is written.

22 Which, ten years down the line, Linux became. To a large extent, it's the GNU project we have to thank for that.

remain available for him to use. Without such insight the project would probably not have amounted to much. In dire straits financially, Stallman even lived for a while at his MIT office.

And so began the history of Free Software. The project was obviously a success, because as early as 1991, when Linus Torvalds started working on his own project, nearly all the tool programs were ready and even the missing Hurd kernel was almost complete. When Linux came along at the right time to fill this gap, Stallman's dream was finally coming true.

Most of the nineties was spent on an Internet high, but people didn't know much about any free operating system. However, under the surface spread of the Internet also fomented the development and distribution of Free Software, because through the Internet more and more hackers could get involved in the worldwide effort of jointly barn-raising Open Source. And, although there was not much being written about Linux in the press at the time, in reality most of the Internet servers in Finland, for instance, were already running on Linux. By the end of the decade, both the press and the corporate world were seriously interested both in Linux and the open development models that had given rise to it.

At this point, a group of leading hackers got together to discuss the situation (not computer criminals, that is, but the leaders of the Free Software community). They realized that their time had finally come. The hacker culture that had almost passed into history was back and it was challenging commercial software companies. The corporate world was genuinely interested in Free Software. But how could they make the most of the situation? How could they get companies to invest in Linux systems? How could they get the software companies to switch to an open development model? And how should they prepare for the inevitable counter assault from Microsoft?

What the hacker fathers decided was that Free Software needed a new brand, a brand which would take a lot of PR work to establish. That's how in early 1998 the term, or brand, *Open Source* was coined.

How did they come to settle on the name *Open Source*? Richard Stallman's term, *Free Software*, had been taking some heat for being ambiguous. The word *free*, which used to refer to freedom, could be taken to mean *free of charge*. Talking about programs for free didn't sound like a good idea, considering these guys wanted to get the software companies involved. And merely having to discuss the semantics of a word is confusing in itself, as it is bound to lead discussion away from the thing that really needed to be talked about. A brand should be short and succinct, not confusing.

Of course, Richard Stallman had to sort out the same semantic problem a lot earlier, and he'd come up with the catchy mnemonic, *free as in speech, not free as in beer*. Free beer is great, but free speech is rather more important. And this was the freedom Stallman liked to speak about – and that was part of the problem. People might have been able to live with the ambiguity of the word *free*, but when it relates to computer programs and somebody starts spouting about freedom of speech, it starts to eat away at their credibility. And that wasn't all. Stallman was also happy to expound his opinion that the *closed* software model was actually unethical!

All this talk was the real reason the term *Open Source* was coined. The other hacker elders had decided to distance themselves from the ideological rhetoric of the otherwise honourable GNU project. That didn't really sit well in interviews with newspapers like the *Wall Street Journal*. A new identity was needed, one that would work both on Wall Street and in software companies. Tangle-haired Richard Stallman was out, and instead they offered the smiling poster boy Linus Torvalds.

But to create this new identity, they needed a new name. Open Source stated clearly what it was all about: the source code was open and available. Openness lead to quality, as Eric Raymond had explained in his essay, 'The Cathedral and the Bazaar'. Open Source equals quality. If you want the best software, give up Windows and use Linux! If you want the cheapest alternative, use Linux! We know nothing of ethics, but we do know what works best when it comes to programming computers: *Open Source*!

The Open Source brand was a phenomenal success. Linus Torvalds was smiling and smiling and smiling on magazine cover after magazine cover. On its first day of trading, the Linux company Red Hat's stock quadrupled. Little by little, companies started using Linux more and more. Netscape become the first closed software to open up its code, becoming the Open-Source-based project called Mozilla. Others have followed, including an OpenOffice word processing program previously known as StarOffice, which is the one I used to write this book. But first and foremost, the press and the public got to know of the concept of Open Source.

But not everybody was happy. Richard Stallman didn't approve of the use of the term Open Source. He felt it was important to understand the ideology behind Free Software, not just settle for 'using what works best'. And although the Open Source camp made its biggest advances outside the hacker community, many within it stayed true to Stallman and the original ideology of Free Software.

The bitterest fights between the supporters of Free Software and those who espouse the term Open Source are happily in the past, but you can still tell which party they belong to by listening for which term they use when speaking of Linux. It's not just any choice of words. It's all about identity and the ideology behind it. And the hackers hold on to those.

What is ethics?

Surprisingly, the struggle between the two camps of Free Software and Open Source leads us to a fascinating question: What is ethics?

The archetype representing the Open Source camp is, of course, Linus Torvalds whose attitude can be described as pragmatic, practical and *engineery*. In addition to this approach being natural to Linus, he also believes his position as leader of the Linux project commits him to being as neutral as possible. That's why he doesn't want to get involved in political issues. His maxim is more or less, *we do what works best, and in programming Open Source is what works best*.

Richard Stallman, father of the Free Software side, considers it very dangerous to limit oneself to such simple thinking. He thinks there is a significant difference between open and closed software development, and this difference influences things as important as equality and the transparency of State administration, but also important technical issues such as data protection and trust. All this leads directly to the conclusion that, more than anything else, the question of the best model for developing software is an ethical one.

So what is ethics?

Mad cow disease – or bovine spongiform encephalopathy (BSE) – was caused by feeding cows a mixture of meal made from the brains and bones of dead cows and sheep. I don't know what's wrong with European farming, but here we go again! Since good brains were going to waste, somebody thought it would be a good idea to feed them back to the cows and save the money farmers would otherwise spend on real feed. A few years later we had mad cow disease and tens of Europeans dead as a result of eating the beef from these cows.

Although Finland was spared this epidemic, which mostly devastated the British farming industry, the crisis was widely discussed here. On a TV chat show, a farmer from the north said that in the early nineties feed which had included brain matter had been offered to farmers in Finland. However, Finnish farmers considered that having cows grow fat on the offal from other cows was completely unethical and they refused to buy the feed.

So, in northern Finland we had a farmer who spoke of what is *ethical*. Today, the infamous 'meat-and-bone meal' is banned throughout Europe. Yet, ten years earlier, farmers in Finland had refused to use it because they didn't think it was *ethical*! And since the meat-and-bone meal had not been used here, Finland was spared mad cow disease and the tragic consequences that followed it in other parts of Europe.

In hindsight, it's easy to say it would have made sense to ban the meat-and-bone meal from the outset. It ought to have been clear to anyone that cattle shouldn't be fed such fodder. If no farmers had ever fed their cows the meat-and-bone meal, Europe would have been spared the unnecessary loss of life and livestock caused by the epidemic. But how could anybody have guessed all that would happen?

A good question! And yet there were farmers who chose not to use the meat-and-bone meal – not for any practical or scientific reason but because they found the idea of it *unethical*. In hindsight, their taking an ethical standpoint saved lives. And in hindsight that's what worked for the best.

In a way, when the adherents of Open Source speak – with political incorrectness – of 'only what works', they are right. But could Richard Stallman have used the same argument in 1984, when the business world was moving only in the direction of closed software? Because the field of software as a whole was so young, there were no facts and practical experiences to draw on to defend either model. So Stallman was forced to talk about ethics. And he was right, but that didn't become apparent until much later.

In a sense, the reason Stallman, too, ended up making his Free Software crusade was that he found that closed software didn't work as well as the free kind. In his essay 'The GNU Project', he tells of an office printer they had in the lab at MIT. Because it was encumbered with a clumsy driver program, using the printer was extremely frustrating. Being a talented programmer, Stallman knew he could easily fix the problem, but the company that sold the printer refused to hand over the source code of its software! This episode affected Stallman's later conclusions.

So we've come full circle. When Linus Torvalds sticks to his 'only what works' line, he is actually talking ethics! Ethical solutions are ethical precisely because they are the right ones. And the right solutions are right because they work.

Part Three

in which there is a balancing act between principles and avarice, Netscape is freed, Stephen King leaves the last pages of a novel unwritten, and you get paid for work.

The business models of a hacker

The fact that the ideology espoused by genuine hackers is vastly different from the mainstream attitude of the software industry poses a very practical challenge. If Open Source programs are handed out for free, what openings can there be for long-term business opportunities?[23] But any talk of ethics is just empty words unless the ideology works in real life. If it doesn't, it is Utopian wishful thinking: it sounds perfectly fine, but it's untenable. This defence follows Linus Torvalds' principle of 'only what works' and a good measure of what works is the corporate world, so that is where we must look to see how viable are the thoughts presented earlier in this book. For the hacker ethic not to be a Utopian dream, we must be able to show that Linux companies, despite working to hacker principles, can make it financially in competition with other companies.

Even when measured on the fast-paced timeline of the IT field, Open Source is relatively new, which means all Open Source companies are still young. It is too soon to judge which are the success stories and which companies will flounder after a strong start. Even so, this part of the book will be devoted to real-life examples of both success and failure in the world of Linux business ideas. The completely new rules of the Linux market can be seen in the innovative ideas spawned by this market. A new situation requires new thinking.

Selling water

Considering that almost all Open Source programs are available on the Internet to be downloaded free, a surprising number of companies have built their business on selling the Linux OS and associated programs. These companies are called *Linux distributions*. Best-known among them are probably Red Hat Linux, SuSE Linux, Mandrake Linux, and in Finland the Finnish-language version called SOT Linux. Only a few years ago all these companies generated most of their revenue by selling Linux CDs packed in colourful cardboard boxes, in the same way as established software companies.

---

23 In reality, Open Source doesn't mean the programs are free of charge, but that the client, i.e. the user, has the right to the source code of the program together with the right to further develop the program and distribute it. These terms prevent the birth of a Microsoft-type monopoly and thereby keep prices reasonable but not necessarily at zero. In practice, you can download most Open Source programs for free, but there is no obligation for them to be made available for free.

This business model can be explained by analogy to water, which is free, yet selling it can be good business. And I don't just mean selling water to people living in deserts. We all buy water daily when we turn on the tap. Even though tap water isn't very expensive, paying our water bills certainly pays for staffing at a water purifying plant, and for a few plumbers too. In addition to tap water, most of us also buy bottles of Evian or some other expensive spring water. So selling water can be a profitable business in more ways than one.

Although there are many Open Source programs available for free on the Internet, it's a lot more practical for users to buy a bunch of CDs and get all the most important programs at once instead of having to spend hours on their slow Internet connection, gathering them for free off the Web. In this, the analogy of selling water is interesting, because on the CD market, too, there are two kinds of compilations. Some companies have specialized in making CDs with as many different programs as possible on them and selling them cheap. This is the tap water of Linux distribution. On the other hand, we have companies like Red Hat that sell CDs under the protection of their own trademark and with their own logos – and the funny thing is, people are happy to pay a little more for a genuine Red Hat Linux rather than buy a no-brand CD with more or less identical content.

In many ways, this *selling-water* business model is a lot like that used by established software companies. In both cases, the business is based on selling software on CDs. However, the similarity is usually only skin-deep. When you buy software from Microsoft, for instance, you don't necessarily buy the CD because you need the CD itself, but because the law says you have to buy it if you want the right to use a particular program. If you have a second computer at home and you want to run the same Microsoft Office software on it, you should buy a second copy of the software on another CD. You don't actually *need* that second CD, because you already have one with exactly the same content, but you have to buy it anyway.

However, Linux distributions that use the *selling-water* business model don't *make* anybody buy anything. If the CD is useful, you can buy it, but if you don't need it (because you can download the software from the Internet) you don't have to buy it and you certainly don't need to buy multiple copies of it. You can use the program anyway, whether or not you have bought the CD. Companies selling such CDs are OK with that and everybody is happy. The mean-spirited business model used by established software companies seems very artificial and a lot of ordinary computer users – laymen, if you will – find it hard to understand why they have to buy multiple copies of an expensive software CD they don't actually need, and really resent it. So, at least selling Linux distribution CDs as CDs seems rather more natural than the various artificial and mean-spirited sanctions imposed by established software companies.

Give software away for free, sell services for a fee

The idea of giving software away for free and selling services for a fee was current by the mid-nineties. In a sense, the *selling-water* business model is one way of realizing this principle.

The main theory behind selling services is very simple. Free software isn't enough for most people, because your average computer user doesn't know how to install the programs, and needs help to get started. In addition to help with installation, many people would also benefit from a few tips on how to use the program. The simplest form of selling services is to provide an easy-to-use and helpful guide along with the software CD. That is, you don't necessarily buy the software CD to get the CD itself, but to get the *User's Guide* that comes with it.

Put that way, it's easy to see how easily a profitable business can be built around a free program. The above example is just the beginning. The really big business is in selling services to large corporations or communities with extensive computer systems. Installing Free Software on the 14,000 computers belonging to the City of Munich is a big job. Then, all the people who use the programs need to be trained. The transfer to a new system must be planned carefully and implemented as smoothly as possible, so as to cause as little disturbance as possible to the actual work being done. Some programs may need to be adapted – or *tailored* as it's known in the trade – to work smoothly with whatever internal information system is already in use. The users will need customer support and the computers will need servicing and updating. Antivirus and other protective software must be kept up to date at all times. And so on ...

The City of Munich is in the process of moving its entire IT infrastructure onto Linux-based systems. At the time of bidding, the contract to provide this *service* to the city was estimated at some EUR 35 million. So it's not really for free!

The services business model isn't really so exotic. Increasingly, all the big IT corporations that used to focus on selling computer hardware and/or software are becoming service consultancies.

Selling services is particularly interesting when it's built around Open Source software, because there is the same threat of monopolization inherent in support services for closed software or closed hardware that there is in the closed programs themselves. If, for instance, you buy an IBM supercomputer and the IBM AIX OS that goes with it, you're very likely indeed to require a bit of help in getting started.[24] Realistically, you have to go to IBM to get that help, because not many other people understand these machines very well – at least not as well as those at IBM. And when it comes to tailoring and updates, you definitely have no other options than IBM, because the source code for these programs is not *open*. Only IBM employees have access to it and can make changes in it.

If you've bought an open system, however, you can get your service wherever you want. If you end up using a computer running Red Hat Linux, for instance, it's likely that you also want to buy the support services from Red Hat, because they are obviously the experts on their own product. But if you don't like their service or you think it's too expensive, you can get the service from any other company you like. There are plenty to choose from – anybody who has studied computer science in the past five years is likely to be able to help you. Tailor-made solutions and updates pose no problems either, because everybody has access to the Linux code.

Such competition is, of course, advantageous to the customer. At the same time, it also seems sensible and somehow natural. It makes sense for you to buy the services you need from wherever you get the best attention. The competition also keeps the companies that sell such services on their toes. The customer or client isn't bound forever to the same service provider just because they once chose to use their system. If the quality of service slackens off, you can always change your provider, which means they have to earn the loyalty of their customers by continuing to provide good service.

---

24 And why wouldn't you? The cheapest IBM supercomputer comes at a reasonable
    $21,645, though you are more likely to want one of the proper machines that cost around
    half a million. The deal includes an operating system and a year's worth of updates, so
    there's also a bit of service thrown in to sweeten the deal.

Another aspect of selling services also seems sensible and natural. When clients buy a service, they are buying work. That's opposed to buying a Microsoft CD, which you don't even need, and which doesn't cause Microsoft to work any harder. It's simply free money that just flows into Microsoft without them really having to work for it. At least services can be billed in some relation to how much work a commission requires. A closed computer program, on the other hand, can be priced arbitrarily and that's usually a losing game for customers and clients.

But selling services is also good for the business providing them. If sales of services are compared to sales of software on CDs – and this holds true whether it's a closed or open program being sold according to the *selling-water* principle – the selling of services generates far more long-lasting clients and therefore more lasting cash flow. A computer program is bought just once, whereas the need for support is usually permanent. Service contracts can even be made on the basis of a monthly fee, which gives a steady cash flow into the company providing the service. In return, the company must do a good job to keep the customer or client happy.

Any company whose business is based on one-off sales is always in a strange relationship to its customers or clients, because they should always try to get them the best possible product, but not so good that they won't be interested in buying a new and improved version of it the following year. This conflict occurs in many fields: for example, in maintaining a balance of fragility and strength in pantyhose for women. However, this has not yet posed a problem for Linux businesses. The Linux world has developed so rapidly in the past few years that Red Hat, for instance, has published two new versions of its Linux distribution in the busiest years. The world of Windows, on the other hand, is so much more mature that the updates published by Microsoft – particularly in the Office family – have seemed to be more like artificial ways of making more money. You should get the latest version, but nobody knows why. Realizing the problem, in the past few years Microsoft have tried to move increasingly into being a service-based industry and charging annual fees.

If you compare the business models of *selling water* and *selling services*, the latter of which is favoured by Linux companies, it is interesting to note that since the nineties all the major Linux companies have been trying to become service companies, yet, until recent years, most of their revenue was coming from sales of CDs packed in colourful boxes. In 2003, there was a clear change. Big jobs like the City of Munich are seriously opening the doors of the services market. Also, old Unix computers in many a company basement are busily being upgraded to Linux. At the same time, increasing numbers of Internet users are getting fast Internet access and have a CD-ROM burning capability, which makes getting Linux off the Internet and making CDs at home increasingly widespread, and thereby minimizing the importance of CD sales.

Of the big Linux companies, Red Hat suddenly decided in the summer of 2003 to stop making its cheap basic Linux. Since then the company has focused entirely on servicing the needs of its well-paying corporate clients, and based on its good accounts, there are enough of those. Red Hat is now selling its Enterprise Linux products wholly on the basis of an annual fee, that is, they've stopped selling cardboard boxes. In January 2004, SuSE was bought by Novell, an old and experienced software business, which means it now has a considerably wider and more experienced services network to offer its clients than does Red Hat. SuSE has made several successful deals with cities in Germany. Mandrake Linux, popular with many home users, has encouraged its customers not to buy CDs but rather to download their Linux from the Internet, provided they spend a corresponding sum on the Mandrake Club service.

Open Source with a catch
(Red Hat Network and SuSE YAST)

Experience has shown that working with a completely open business model has proved tricky for many Linux companies. As previously explained, the clients of a Linux company are free to demand the best and cheapest service, and to switch to other providers who may offer a better service. This puts Linux companies on the spot and many of them have tried to make things easier for themselves by including some sort of catch in their service agreements, something that will keep customers loyal despite the openness. We'll now take a look at two examples of this.

Red Hat is the best-known company selling the Linux OS and services, so in many ways it is fitting for this review of Linux companies to start with them. As a company Red Hat has always been strongly behind the Free

Software ideology, and from the start they published all their own products under the same open GPL (General Public Licence) under which Linux is published. Despite this, there are some catches to be found in the company history.

Until the year 2003, Red Hat's best-known and most important product was the Linux operating system itself. Most users copied it freely from the Internet, but there were also a lot of other people who bought Red Hat Linux CDs from the stores. Even so, for a long time now Red Hat has worked to increase its revenue by providing services. And because the company employs some of the most talented programmers, or hackers, of the Linux world, the company's consultancy services have a certain credibility. The well-known Internet store Amazon, for one, trusted Red Hat consultants when porting its Web servers to a Linux platform.

Despite their hard work to improve their income from selling services, Red Hat's biggest revenue-generator in its first years of business was from selling Linux on CDs. But because it was also possible to download the same content directly from the Internet for free, many users acquired their Linux OS that way.

Inherent in the logistics of CD production is a certain difficulty in the selling of CDs, which was financially unfavourable to Red Hat. Once the contents of a CD have been compiled – i.e. Linux and other compatible programs – they can be published in digital form on the Internet the very next day. However, for the physical CD-ROM the journey to the retail outlets would only then be getting started. The time-consuming business of manufacturing the CDs, printing the covers, and transporting the finished product to the shops meant that by the time the CDs were available for sale they were often a month or even two months behind the identical software already spreading via the Internet. With such a long delay even those Red Hat users who would have preferred to buy a CD ended up downloading Red Hat Linux from the Internet for free because they didn't want to wait.

At one point, Red Hat tried to bypass this problem by delaying the Internet release of its latest versions. The new versions were distributed only after the physical CDs had been in retail stores for a couple of weeks. Although we can appreciate the logic behind this artificial delay, it did provoke some criticism. After all, it could be considered mean-spirited. Also, it may well have been an unprofitable tactic for Red Hat itself. Since Linux was then developing at an amazing pace, a delay of up to two months was quite a long time. Holding back the new version meant that their product was already out of date by the time it was published. The tactic also gave an edge to other Linux distributors, who released their own versions on the Internet without delay. After a while, even Red Hat seemed unable to believe in its own plan, and so gave it up.

In the Internet era, the most important task of any operating system provider has become the quick finding and fixing of bugs in their system. Flaws in programs can be used to break into computers, which is why it is important to fix them quickly and efficiently. In the past few years, almost all the viruses that have spread in the Windows world have made use of bugs either in Windows itself or in the e-mail application Outlook. Linux has proved more reliable than Windows in this, and has therefore not had the same kind of viral epidemics, but in theory all operating systems are similarly at risk. That makes the fixing of faults as soon as they're found one of the mainstays of computer security. In practice, this responsibility falls on the supplier of the OS, whether the company in question is Red Hat, Microsoft, or anyone else.

The flawlessness of the Red Hat system is based on the use of the up2date program and subscribing to the corresponding Red Hat Network service. For a client who has joined the Red Hat Network all the available updates are just a click or two away.

Red Hat's business is now wholly based on the sale of annual subscription fees for joining the Red Hat Network. The operating system sold by Red Hat is no longer even itemized as a separate product; getting the OS and a year's worth of updates is always a package deal. Pricing is also based on an annual fee, not on the one-off purchase of a CD. Today, Red Hat focuses entirely on its Enterprise products, which are seriously pricey. The annual fee per computer varies from the cheapest versions at $179 to $349 dollars to big computer server versions at $1,499 to $18,000. In addition to consultancy deals with big clients, the most important source of revenue for Red Hat is the up2date program and the Red Hat Network subscription fees.

The up2date program is closely tied to the Red Hat Network and its annual fees. Many other Linux distributions and the correspondingly simple update programs allow installation and updates through a third party. This benefits consumers, because it allows them easy installation and upkeep of the more exotic software which doesn't come with the Linux distribution itself. And that really is what Open Source is all about: for the consumer to have the freedom to build their computer from whatever programs best suit their needs. But this would mean that Red Hat's customers could update their entire operating system from some third party, and thereby do away with the need for the expensive Red Hat Network contract. Of course you can update Red Hat Linux without the up2date program, but all the alternatives require some amount of computer skill. The only way officially sanctioned by Red Hat is to use their Red Hat Network.

By forcing users of its up2date program to pay expensive annual fees Red Hat has, surprisingly enough, elected to get its revenue from a rather aggressive and very much un-open catch. Although the source code for the up2date program itself is open and follows the principles of Open Source, its use is surprisingly closed, considering the history and principles of Red Hat. It's not just about money – any business needs to make a profit – it's more about the mean-spirited limiting of choices. In order to make a profit, Red Hat has tied the up2date program to its own servers and thereby excluded the rest of the Internet and all the potential on offer there. Which means a Red Hat user is forced to make a choice that is disadvantageous to them. If you use Red Hat, you must get all your software through Red Hat. If you need programs that Red Hat doesn't offer, you have to make do without them. Naturally, it's possible to install programs from other sources than Red Hat Network, but because the up2date software doesn't support them, the installation and upkeep will cause unnecessary hassle.[25]

For the sake of comparison, we'll give all the companies presented in this part of the book a brief evaluation. Or perhaps verdict would be a better word. So what's the verdict for Red Hat? Among Linux companies, Red Hat is one of the strongest proponents of the Free Software ideology. All Red Hat's own software is also published under the GPL licence. Red Hat Network's closed nature is somewhat in conflict with hacker ethics, but is acceptable – barely.

Switching to a service-oriented business model and corporate products has been a financially viable strategy. In the fall of 2003, Red Hat published its first ever profit result and has stayed clearly in the black ever since. In

---

25 To clarify, in the free Fedora Core Linux which Red Hat has published since 2003 mostly for hobby and test use, the up2date program has been changed so that users can freely add other websites from which software can be installed and updated. At the time of writing, all actual Red Hat products aimed at businesses are still tied to the Red Hat Network service.

the autumn of 2004, the company generated a profit of $12 million, which is a lot considering the turnover is only $46 million. After a strong growth, Red Hat has made a hit with its Red Hat Network, and has taken its place in the world of grown-up companies, where you don't get along on fancy technology alone, you also have to run a profitable business.

Verdict: Financially successful company whose actions can stand a hacker-ethical inspection, but there's still room to improve.

SuSE LINUX is a Linux company with strong German roots. Its history is as long and venerable as that of Red Hat, and it is generally considered to be number two in the competition between Linux distributions. At the beginning of the millennium, SuSE equalled Red Hat in turnover and number of employees, but then had some financial problems and almost halved its staff. The company stayed afloat, thanks to support from IBM.

Today, SuSE is seen as IBM's foremost Linux partner, and IBM's database and mainframe architectures are usually first to be supported by SuSE products. SuSE Linux is also supported by all the other big software companies, such as database manufacturer Oracle and super computer manufacturers Cray and SGI. With this in mind, it's easy to believe that SuSE, like Red Hat, employs some of the best Linux programmers in the world.

It made quite a splash in the Linux world when, in the autumn of 2003, the old IT giant Novell announced they had bought SuSE for $210 million. Novell is known for its NetWare operating system, which in the early nineties was the most popular OS for company intranet file and print servers. Although the company still has a large and loyal customer base, it has lost market share to Microsoft since the late nineties when many people saw Novell as something of an historic remnant in the IT business. However, in 2003 Novell decided to go with Linux and bought in top knowledge by first acquiring Ximian (more of which later) then a couple of months later the number two Linux distribution SuSE. IBM stayed in the equation, because part of the SuSE deal was that the company made a $50 million investment in Novell. Overnight, SuSE LINUX had become the product of an established, venerable and, importantly, a financially stable IT company, and once again Novell became a hot name in supplying netowrk servers.

The story of SuSE's survival teaches a lesson that has wider application. If you're a talented professional, you'll always land on your feet. In this instance, SuSE had become such an important expert partner for IBM, that Big Blue simply couldn't afford to let the company sink. IBM needed SuSE to realize its own Linux strategy and with IBM's support, the company survived its other less than profitable experiments.

The Novell deal was basically about the same thing. Because Linux is an operating system that is both open and free, there's no reason to pay hundreds of millions of dollars just to have your own Linux version. That wasn't what it was about: it was about Novell paying for and getting top-notch knowledge of Linux – and, if you want to know my opinion, they got it cheap.

As with Red Hat, the two most important sources of revenue for SuSE have been consultancy and the sale of CDs. Unlike Red Hat, SuSE continued to sell the packages suitable for the ordinary consumer.

The strategy SuSE originally chose for its CD sales has been severely criticized. In addition to the freely distributable open Linux programs, SuSE Linux comes with an installation and administration program created by SuSE and known as YAST, the licensing terms of which don't fall under the definition of Open Source. The installation program, and therefore the entire CD, can be copied freely, but you mustn't sell it. That is how SuSE prevents cheap clones being made of its Linux, something that always eats up some of the profits in other Linux companies. Furthermore, and unusually for a Linux distribution, SuSE CDs cannot be copied from the Internet, which means more users of SuSE have been forced to buy CDs to get what they want than have those using other Linux distributions.

Though SuSE has the full and legal right to define the licensing terms of its own programs as strictly as it pleases, I think it is reasonable to ask how they can justify putting in such restrictions when the rest of the contents on their CDs is Open Source and therefore freely available and free for the company to use. Where is reciprocity? And should we understand the SuSE strategy to mean that the second-largest Linux distributor doesn't think Open Source programs can really be used for profitable business?

Despite the well-earned criticism, SuSE has got off rather lightly and has always been a respected member of the Open Source community. Caldera, for instance, met with far harder resistance when they tried a similar strategy, and that company has since disowned its Linux enterprises entirely, having already burnt all the bridges behind it. The reason the SuSE strategy was received so much more kindly is that SuSE is actively involved in the development of the Linux kernel, the KDE windowing environment, and several other important Open Source projects. These weigh more on the good side of the scales than stepping away from the Open Source principle in one instance.

After Novell bought SuSE, the company published the above-mentioned YAST program under the same GPL licence as Linux, which means the SuSE catch is now history and we can forget all about the little flaw that once existed in an otherwise excellent Linux distribution. In this review, we've been looking at the old SuSE, with the catch still in place, and the verdict is therefore based on that. Novell's solutions are the SuSE of the future and will have to be evaluated by others.

Verdict: After surviving its financial troubles SuSE is building its business as a consultancy with excellent know-how, particularly in exotic mainframe environments. As a company SuSE shows how a skilled professional will always have work. The company's Linux distribution is popular, but the realization of the whole package (prior to the Novell buy-out) unfortunately failed our ethical criteria. Whereas the Red Hat catch barely scraped through, the SuSE catch, just as barely, fails it.

The patron and the artist (O'Reilly and Larry Wall, Transmeta and Linus Torvalds, KDE)

One way many Open Source hackers use to support themselves somewhat resembles the relationship between a Renaissance artist and his rich patron. Perhaps the modern version is sponsorship, but the analogy of patron and artist is a better description. The best example of this *patron-and-artist* model is the long relationship between Larry Wall, creator of the popular programming language Perl, and his former employer, the publishing house O'Reilly & Associates. One would be justified in wondering what the creator and developer of an Open Source programming language was doing as a full-time employee in a publishing house.

O'Reilly has become known as the publisher of top-notch computer guides. The company's trademark is to print an exotic animal on its book covers. For example, *Programming Perl*, the guide to Perl, has a camel on its front cover, which is why this Perl programmers' bible has been dubbed *the camel book*.

In the early nineties, the camel book had become compulsory reading for every Perl programmer. Tim O'Reilly, the CEO of the publishing house, realized that the more Perl programmers there were, the more camel books O'Reilly & Associates would sell – so whatever was good for Perl would be good for O'Reilly. Putting his thoughts into action, Tim gave Larry Wall a full-time job to develop Perl while, of course, writing a new edition of the camel book on the side. In addition to this mutually beneficial symbiotic relationship, it was also good PR for the publishers to hire a well-known leader of the Open Source community. O'Reilly has subsequently become the book purveyor not only to Perl programmers but also to the whole Open Source community, supplying programming guides and other kinds of computer literature.

A somewhat similar relationship existed between Linus Torvalds and his former employer Transmeta, which is neither a Linux nor an Open Source company but a manufacturer of low-energy computer processors. When Linus got his degree from the University of Helsinki in 1997, Transmeta hired the undisputed leader of the Linux world and gave him free reign to use his working hours to develop Linux.

Although Transmeta itself had no use for Linux, hiring the world's best-known programmer was a smart move. No amount of money could have bought them such an effective marketing campaign. Media interest was only heightened by the fact that Transmeta had yet to publish a single product and was keeping all plans for its future a secret. It was even uncertain whether or not the company actually made processors or were up to something entirely different. By the time their first processors were made, everybody was bursting with curiosity, so much so that when the company held a press conference it was front-page news in the entire IT press, which meant there was no need for an advertising campaign.

But putting Linus on the payroll was not just charity, nor even a simple marketing gimmick for Transmeta. In principle, Transmeta's new processors were compatible with the processors used in Intel's x86 architecture. And since Linus Torvalds' Linux system had been made for those particular Intel processors, he was naturally one of the world's best authorities on the x86 architecture. Which means he was probably irreplaceable for Transmeta in solving various technical problems, although by his own admission he spent more than half his working day tinkering with his hobby, Linux.

It may not be hard to find patrons eager to support the best programmer in the world. But how about your average unknown hackers? Will somebody want to employ them? Even though the patron-and-artist model probably works best with the hacker stars, there are rank-and-file members of the Open Source community who have managed to make a living in a similar way.

Quanta Plus is an HTML editor that's part of the KDE windowing environment – or, more simply, it's a program you use to make web pages. The two main developers of the program are Eric Laffoon of the US and Andras Mantia of Hungary. Eric's day job is to grow and sell catnip, which apparently cats like so much it's possible to make a living out of growing it. In addition to supporting his own family, Eric sends some of his catnip revenue to Andras, who in turn works full-time on Quanta Plus and other KDE programs. The two men have calculated that this arrangement is more efficient than if both of them tried to develop Quanta Plus in addition to having day jobs. Of course, the difference in the standard of living between Eastern Europe and the US is what makes this particular collaboration possible. But irrespective of world economy, Eric is a true patron who puts money into the KDE project rather than contributing his free time.

KDE has also had a lot of positive publicity through a program called Adopt-a-Geek, a project initiated by KDE activist Scott Wheeler. The whole thing started with the observation that many industrious KDE programmers are students – either from Eastern Europe or from otherwise disadvantaged backgrounds – who do their valuable volunteer work on slow old computers simply because they're the best they can afford. The Adopt-a-Geek program strives to support these poorest of KDE programmers by supplying them with more efficient hardware to enable them to work more efficiently. Although the Adopt-a-Geek project only supplies computers and parts, not money, it is one example of how users of KDE software can help satisfy the material needs of the people who make the programs.[26]

Verdict: The *patron-and-artist* model, or sponsorship, has proved itself a workable way of putting food on the table for an Open Source hacker, but is probably best suited to the famous hacker stars than for your average code merchant. Ethically the model naturally scores an A+. It doesn't just pass ethical review, it practically oozes hacker ethics and the joy of sharing.

---

26 http://devel-home.kde.org/~wheeler/adopt-a-geek/

Pay for work (Germany and Kroupware)

What would you pay somebody to do if not work? The twists and turns of the market economy are wonderful, but even amidst all the brilliant business ideas of the techno boom at the turn of the millennium, there are still people out there who actually support themselves by honest work! This notion, which is so self-evident it could sound sarcastic, is an example of the *selling-services* business model. Established software companies initiate and make a computer program which they then sell packaged in colourful boxes, whereas in the *pay-for-work* model software is specifically commissioned. It works something like this: brilliant Open Source programs are available on the Internet free for anyone to use. If, however, what you need is not yet out there, programmers can write it for you – provided you pay, of course.

One example of the successful implementation of this model was the *Kroupware* project commissioned by the Federal Republic of Germany. In the summer of 2002, Germany commissioned a groupware solution running on Linux and the corresponding client or desktop software for use on both Linux and Windows from three companies closely associated with the KDE project (German Efrakon and Intevation, and the Swedish Klarälvdalens datakonsult).

A groupware solution is the kind of e-mail program that contains not just e-mail but other functions that are useful in an office, such as a calendar, contacts and, in some cases, chat groups. The best known groupware solutions used by companies are Microsoft's Exchange and IBM's Lotus Notes. Although there are a number of e-mail server programs available for Linux, nobody had yet made this type of multi-tasking tool. But the German authorities wanted to take their groupware needs into the world of Open Source.

The three companies with the winning tender named the project Kroupware.[27] They decided to build the software around well-known Open Source programs, such as Apache's web server, the e-mail server Postfix, the OpenLDAP directory server and the IMP Webmail. The desktop software was created from existing and well-functioning KDE project modules, the e-mail program, calendar and contacts, which with a little work

---

27 There is a tradition in the KDE project to give all programs names beginning with the letter K, hence from *groupware* you get *Kroupware*. What was originally a fun idea has paled over the years.

could be made into an entity resembling Microsoft Outlook. Naturally, some functions had to be created from scratch, but a lot of the work had already been done and could be put to direct use, which meant the Kroupware project was completed in record time in the summer of 2003. The resulting software was finally called *Kolab*.

Finishing such a complex software project within one year is somewhat unheard of in the IT world. Even more incredible is that the work was done by three relatively small and unknown consultancies. The fast pace of the work was only possible because the project could build so much on top-quality Open Source work that had already been done.[28]

The Kroupware project breaks with familiar market-economy mechanisms in an interesting way. The Federal Republic of Germany got the groupware application it wanted, but because the Kolab software is Open Source anyone who subsequently needs a good groupware solution for a Linux platform can copy it for free from the Internet! Is it fair that a software solution paid for by the German taxpayers could then be used by others free of charge?

Offhand, that may seem unfair, but in the world of Open Source such an outcome is standard practice. Since the beginning of hacking, Open Source hackers have always made programs *to suit their own needs*. With little interest in who else may or may not benefit from their work, their primary interest has essentially been to solve their own problems. As a client, the Federal Republic of Germany accepted this logic, and they aren't likely to have any reason to complain. Not only did they get what they wanted, they got a high-quality solution, they got it cheap, and they got it fast. What could be unfair about that?

Actually, Germany didn't have to pay for all of Kolab. After all, most of the Kolab software was made up of existing Open Source programs, the creation of which required many thousands of man-hours worth of blood, sweat and tears – or rather, loads of excited hacker spirit. For all this work – worth millions, if not billions – Germany didn't have to pay a single pfenning, nor for that matter even a single cent.

It is important to keep that in mind if we are to understand how Open Source works at its best. If we spend all our time jealously guarding how others might end up with more than we do, life can grind to a halt while all

---

28 Hackers like to quote Isaac Newton, who wrote, 'If I see further, it is because I stand on the shoulders of giants.'

available time is diverted into sorting out disputes and backing out of dead ends. If instead we all focus on solving our own problems, everybody can be a winner.

Verdict: The *pay-for-work* business model that has proved to work very well is completely consistent with hacker ethics and utilises the strengths of Open Source. It's also worth mentioning that all the other models we've looked at have their financial roots in something other than programming. That is, their main business is consultancy, and programming is more or less a hobby done on the side. In the Kroupware project, however, programmers were actually paid to write code, which seems a very healthy thought! The *pay-for-work* principle appeals to everybody's common sense, particularly when we've seen the number of millionaires, on paper, created by the technology explosion.

However, the Kroupware project does leave some questions unanswered. The Federal Republic of Germany is a big enough client to be able to finance such a commission single-handed. But what about smaller clients? Must smaller companies and consumers wait for crumbs to fall from the tables of the big corporations and nation states, or could the same model work on a smaller scale? Such questions are what we'll look at next.

Stephen King, the tip model, and the job market (Stephen King, Roger Williams, SourceForge, Kolab, JBoss)

In 2000, the well-known horror writer Stephen King conducted some interesting experiments in Internet publishing. Although they weren't Open Source projects, King clearly understood the dynamics between immaterial work and the Internet so well that there is much we can learn from him.

King made history in the spring of 2000 by publishing his novel *Riding the Bullet* in digital form only. It was the first time a well-known author had written a book not intended for printed publication. The vendors of various eBook solutions and programs made the most of this opportunity, and old news clippings remind us of all 'the death of printed books' stories.[29]

The cost of publishing a book in digital form is of course far less than having it printed. This, and marketing reasons, allowed King's book to be

---

29 Despite all that was said in 2000, three years later Stephen King's story *Riding the Bullet* was published in the printed collection *Everything's Eventual*.

sold for as little as $2.50. In the first 24 hours, an amazing 40,000 copies of the book were sold. I don't know what sales figures King is used to, but the press at least saw this as a huge success and the makers of eBook products pointed to it as proof of – what else? – 'the death of printed books'.

However, it seems King wasn't altogether pleased with the experiment. Despite the fact that the eBook files had been protected with some childishly simple copy protection mechanisms, crackers quickly broke through them, and pirated versions of the book quickly spread on the Internet. Even though the webstores Amazon.com and Barnes&Noble.com were, by this time, distributing the book *free* on their websites for advertising purposes, the existence of pirated versions seemed to annoy Stephen King enormously.

His readers weren't particularly happy about the various eBook formats, either. Because of the copy protection it was impossible to get a printout of the book from the eBook programs. It could only be read while sitting at a computer, which effectively prevented anyone from curling up on the couch or hiding under the covers at night to read King's latest exciting story. And there was a further irony to his use of copy-prevention techniques. Because there was nothing to prevent anyone from printing out the *pirated* editions of the story, they were inevitably more user-friendly than the official eBook editions.

The eBook hype has since faded away, and despite all the doomsday prophecies the printed book has not died, because it is still far more enjoyable to read a story printed on paper than it is to read it on a computer screen. Today, however, many people continue to work on creating more functional systems to prevent copying, apparently in the belief that readers will eventually want to buy books they can't read in the comfort of their favourite position.

Despite his disappointment, King had sufficient pioneering spirit to go ahead with a new Internet experiment the following summer. This time he chose to publish his work on his own website, thereby bypassing all established publishers. Coincidentally the story, called *The Plant*, was all about a murderous vampire plant striking terror into the hearts of the employees of a publishing house. Meanwhile, Stephen King's experiment struck terror into the lives of real publishers, who feared that if it succeeded it could undermine the very existence of the publishing industry.

After his disappointing eBook experiences, King intended to turn things upside-down with this book. He published the first two chapters on the

Internet without any complicating attempts to prevent copying – this was a straightforward text on a straightforward website. However, the text wasn't free, as readers were asked to pay one dollar per chapter they read. If a sufficient number of readers paid up, King said he would finish the story, one chapter at a time.

King's idea was somewhat similar to the Kroupware *pay-for-work* model described earlier. He accepted that many people would read his work for free. That didn't matter to him, provided enough readers also paid. He reasoned that if people were willing to pay, he would do the work.

This foray into self-publishing didn't get as good a reception as the eBook experiment earlier in the year, but in the first week some 152,132 eager fans had visited the site and read the first chapter. Of them some 116,200 had also paid a dollar. This met the terms King had stipulated, so, to his own surprise, he had to write more of this horror story set in the publishing world.

By the time he reached chapter six, however, the excitement had waned. Only some 40,000 people had bothered to read the chapter, and half of them hadn't paid their dollar. So, all of a sudden, King dropped the project that had got off to such a good start.

Of course, the failure of *The Plant* is somewhat disappointing to those who seek an open Web community. If a popular writer like King couldn't earn enough from Internet publishing, who could?

But at least some of the blame can be laid at King's own door. The project might have done better had King had a greater understanding of the mechanisms of Open Source. As it was, his experiment resembled the practices of the Open Source community only by chance, as he probably didn't know about Linux and hadn't learned from it and the flourishing businesses growing up around it. For example, the Stephen King site used the word *thieves* to refer to those who read his story without paying. However, when it comes to marketing, abusing your own readers may not be the smartest thing to do. The experiment also gave the impression that although King didn't really mind that the number of paying readers had dwindled, he actively resented that a growing number of people were reading it for free. Also, at some point, for some incomprehensible reason the first chapter was removed from the site, which virtually guaranteed that no new readers would ever start reading the book. So, there was a sense of a certain lack of openness in the project, which may have influenced the readers and made them apprehensive.

One can't help feeling that King was never fully committed to the project. He had actually written the first two chapters, with which he'd started the whole process, some 20 years earlier. Apparently, he found his incomplete and unpublished text in the attic and published it on the Internet as an experiment. Only when he unexpectedly found that readers were willing to pay for what they'd read, did he bother to write another four chapters, but that was it.

Enjoying the view of hindsight a little longer, we can see that the book publishing project may have worked better if it hadn't been chopped about so much. It seems only natural that the number of paying customers would decrease after the first flurry of excitement, particularly after the first part of the book was removed from his website. It would probably have worked better if customers had been asked to pay a slightly larger sum up front, in either two or at the most three instalments.

Whatever the best way to do it may have been, there is at least one thing to be learned from King: if you write horror fiction, don't ever sell your readers half a book. Readers who were disappointed by King's decision not to finish the book were crushing in their criticism. For some reason King didn't seem to have anticipated that the thousands of readers – who by then had paid seven dollars for part of the book – would be angry when they were denied the end of the exciting story. The anger wasn't exactly dissipated by the promise King had made in the summer that if he ended up writing more than the first two chapters he wouldn't leave the book unfinished. So, the experiences of *The Plant* project may not be very encouraging, but they do serve as a warning: if you cheat your customers, they usually get angry.

Another interesting experiment in Internet publishing was that of *The Metamorphosis of Prime Intellect*, an eight-chapter novel by Roger Williams. Unlike Stephen King, Williams was an unknown and unpublished author, who despite numerous attempts had failed to get a publisher for his novel. His solution was to publish it on the Internet. Although technically, his publishing venture failed to meet the criteria of the Open Source ideology, Williams' approach to Web publishing was rather more positive and open than King's had been. It was published in its entirety, and could be read and copied freely. Williams offered those who liked the novel the chance to give him a tip through the PayPal service.

Later on, Williams wrote about the experience in the article 'The Tip Jar as Revenue Model: A Real-World Experiment'. He not only studied the financial side of the matter, but also stated that for an unknown writer like himself, just having readers was a big thing.[30]

But how did the novel fare?

According to Williams, some 5,000 to 10,000 people read the novel to the end. That's not bad for a first novel by an unknown writer! And he received $760 in tips. Although Williams was happy with his success, he did conclude that the tip jar didn't really cover his rent or groceries.

At the turn of the millennium, somewhat similar Open Source experiments were being carried out in relation to computer programs. But hey, what experiments weren't being done around that time? More than one company actually tried to bring makers and users of Open Source software together in a sort of virtual *job market*. Programmers could use such sites to publicise the sort of program they were currently developing, and interested people or potential consumers could use the site to offer financial support for a particular programmer. Any consumers interested in specifically commissioning software could use such sites to offer the sum of money they were willing to pay. After which other *buyers* interested in the same type of program could commit to the project by paying whatever sum they felt was appropriate. In theory, for a programmer looking for work, all the pledges would provide a nice sum of money once the software in question was finished.

Not one of these projects ever got beyond their initial start-up.[31] Perhaps they were ahead of their time, but more likely the model itself was simply bad. For one thing, the job markets didn't seem to be of any interest to the hacker community. Hackers were already busy with all their existing projects. They preferred to do something they found really interesting without remuneration than to take on something they found boring for mere money.

In early 2004, by far the most popular host of Open Source projects, SourceForge, began offering programmers who used their service the chance

---

30   http://www.kuro5hin.org/story/2003/4/27/195833/305

31   Actually, they failed so dismally that nobody even remembers the names these projects had during their brief existence, which is why this is an anonymous anecdote.

to receive financial donations through the PayPal service with, of course, a percentage of the tips going to SourceForge itself as their commission.[32]

SourceForge's *tip-model* way of financing programmers of Open Source projects differs from the failed job markets in that their first and foremost aim is not to handle transactions of money. SourceForge's real business is to offer programmers the tools they need for their work together with providing a channel for distributing their programs. The chance to support the creator of your favourite software is just an added bonus, not something that lies at the heart of operations.

The success of SourceForge, as compared to the failed job markets, provides us with a good lesson, particularly for future entrepreneurs in the IT business. In the *job-market* model, the most important thing was money, with programming taking second place. On the other hand, new projects are started every day in SourceForge, and nobody says anything about money. Successful projects get some tips – some more, some less. The same thing is clear across the field of IT: there are those who have fancy business plans, and there are those who work.

What was true for Williams' *tip-jar* experiments also holds true for the tips at SourceForge: some money comes in, which is nice, but not enough to support oneself, let alone a family. So does *pay-for-work* really not work on a small scale, especially if one actually needs the amount paid to correspond to a regular salary?

There are some examples of the *pay-for-work* model being implemented successfully for clients smaller than Germany. Almost immediately after the completion of the Kolab 1 project, some companies started asking questions about it in the hope of realizing features that the Germans hadn't thought to order. The businesses that had originally worked on the Kolab project then pulled together the companies asking these questions, and the interested parties pooled their money to finance the next version of the project, Kolab 2. This may be the first time an Open Source project has been realized as a *shared commission* for a consortium of several smaller clients.

JBoss, the company that develops the Java application server of the same name, works in a similar way. The Java application server itself is such a big and complicated piece of software that there aren't many companies willing or able to single-handly pay for the whole thing. That's not how it's come to be either. JBoss has been available on the Internet under the Open

---

32   http://sourceforge.net/

Source principle for years, and has been developing over time. Clients using JBoss are usually happy with it as it is, but every once in a while somebody needs an added feature of some kind. When that happens, they can commission the JBoss company to write the code for it (or commission some other programming company to do the job, because the source code is open and available), and little by little this further develops the JBoss application server. So, horror fiction may not sell well piecemeal, but that seems to work fine for developing Java application servers.

Although the *pay-for-work* model doesn't seem to work at the small consumer level, it seems you don't have to be an economic power the size of Germany to make it work for you.

Verdict: The *pay-for-work* model is a beautiful thought, but so far there's been no evidence to suggest that it works for products aimed at the private citizen or other small consumers. However, it seems that it can work extremely well for medium-sized companies upwards.

Dual licensing (MySQL, Trolltech Qt)

Possibly the most financially successful strategy for Open Source software has been the so-called *dual licensing* of it, particularly the way it is employed by companies making 'low level' tool-type software.

MySQL Ab is a Swedish company known for its popular database program, which is particularly liked for data storage of web pages that run on a Linux platform. The MySQL database can be downloaded for free from the Internet under the same GPL licensing system as Linux. Another option is to buy it under licence for $500. But why would anybody choose to pay 500 bucks for something they can get for free?

Some people want to pay for it to avoid having to commit themselves to the terms of Open Source. The General Public Licence (GPL) requires programmers who use some GPL licensed code or program in any of their software to also publish their own work under the GPL, source code and all.[33] Which is why the programmers who make closed programs can't use

---

33 Not all Open Source software is published under such strict terms. Many Open Source programs or parts of them can also be used in closed software. However, software such as the Linux kernel and MySQL which are published under the GPL licence do not allow this.

the free Open Source version of MySQL, but have to pay $500 for a so-called 'commercial licence'. These customers are usually pretty happy with their purchase, because $500 is not a steep price to pay for a good database product.

For MySQL this arrangement has clearly worked brilliantly. The existence of the free GPL version of MySQL helped make it one of the world's most popular databases. Being well-known is obviously important for any product, but for a programmer's tool it's particularly important that programmers learn to use the program. If a software company employee has already used MySQL for free to create the database for the web pages of the local kennel club, he or she is likely to want to use it as part of the company's closed software project rather than have to learn how to use another database program.

The existence of the GPL version has also speeded up the development of the database. In accordance with the principles of Open Source, many programmers outside the MySQL company have improved the database software, making the company's product improve 'by itself'. In this way the hacker community pays in free labour and user feedback what the manufacturers of closed software must pay for in money.

Trolltech, who developed the popular Qt user interface library, employed the same business model. A user interface library offers programmers the basic building blocks of computer programs – including such things as push buttons, menus, text fields and scroll bars – with which to build the actual software.

One of the strengths of Qt is that it can be used to program software for both Windows and Linux. That makes it a good choice – out of very few – for programmers who want their program to work on as many operating systems as possible.

The Qt library forms the basis of the KDE desktop environment which is so popular for computers running Linux. With KDE, one can freely use the Qt library version published under the terms of the GPL licence. But, like MySQL, Trolltech also sells a licensed version of Qt for use as building blocks in closed programs. The benefits of this arrangement are the same as those for MySQL. The GPL version of Qt gives it visibility and cachet, while the hackers of the KDE community are an important resource in its development. They give feedback on Qt and often also develop it further, and the improvements they make also benefit the commercial Qt.

Dual licensing raises the interesting ethical question of how these companies would fare in a world that is 100 per cent Open Source. Far from topical, the question is nonetheless relevant for those who believe that the Open Source model is fundamentally better than the mean-spirited restrictions of closed software. If the closed software model is so bad that nobody should use it, then what would happen to those companies that make their money from the makers of closed programs? And is it really kosher to support openness and fight mean-spiritedness, while still recommending this *dual licensing* business model?

So far, there doesn't seem to be any good answer to the question. The truth is that, for now at least, dual licensing works very well and seems to satisfy all parties. It supports and provides well for companies like MySQL and Trolltech. The makers of closed programs get high-quality tools at a good price. And the Open Source programmers get the same tools on terms they feel fine with. And there's the added bonus that development of Open Source programs is partly financed by funds from the makers of closed programs, i.e. the opposition.

So everybody is happy and, frankly, although the question remains unanswered nobody seems to care.

Verdict: Dual licensing, as used by MySQL and Trolltech, is arguably the most successful business model of the Open Source world. In addition to these two companies, many others like them have used it successfully. However, this model doesn't suit all. In particular, it doesn't seem to work well with software intended for the end user, as all the companies that use this model are selling products – either programming libraries or databases – to other programmers. The model passes the hacker ethical review, although the question of how companies that use dual licensing would do in a wholly Open Source economy remains to be seen.

Playing for both teams
(Ximian Evolution, CodeWeavers, Transgaming)

Ximian employed a model very similar to dual licensing to license its Evolution e-mail program. For lack of a better description, we'll call this model *playing for both teams*. A company using this model follows in part the principles of Open Source, and in part the rules of the established software industry.

The history of Ximian is closely associated with GNOME, the other Linux desktop environment. Miguel de Icaza, who founded GNOME, also helped to found Ximian, and most of the other key players in that company are also leaders of the GNOME project. Before Ximian, the Mexican de Icaza revealed his sense of humour by styling himself 'peasant farmer' at Linux conferences – a title that hardly does justice to a programming genius on a par with Linus Torvalds.

Most of Ximian's work has been connected to improving, one way or another, the use of Linux on workstations. Ximian's position among the other Linux companies has been curious because in many ways it resembles others, such as Red Hat and SuSE, yet Ximian is not actually a Linux distribution. It's main product Ximian Desktop is designed to be installed on top of somebody else's Linux – a typical combination might be Red Hat Linux with Ximian. In recent years, the company also coordinated and was the most important contributor to the development of Microsoft Mono, which is an Open Source version of the new Microsoft .NET platform. And this is what made Ximian known outside the world of Linux.

In August 2003, Ximian was acquired by Novell, one of the grand old IT companies. As was the case with SuSE, this again shows that an expert is always worth paying for. Because Ximian used to be a private company, no figures were ever made public when it was sold, so any estimates of its profit can only ever be guesswork. Apparently, the largest source of revenue has been the Red Carpet service connected to Ximian Desktop, which its users employ to make installing and updating programs easy (cf. Red Hat Network). However, it is clear that Novell didn't buy Ximian to acquire any single product but rather to get a lot of Linux expertise in one go – just as they did with SuSE. So, another business model that has proven itself in the Open Source world is to demonstrate your skills as a Free Software programmer until somebody hires you or – as with Ximian – buys your company.

But getting back to our test case, one of the Ximian products is the e-mail program Evolution. Ximian took it upon itself to develop an e-mail client because the lack of this was one of the biggest obstacles to the corporate world moving from Windows to Linux.[34] When Evolution was ready, it was published according to Open Source principles, which meant for instance that anybody could use it for free.

Alongside Evolution, Ximian also published a product called Connector for Microsoft Exchange, which made it possible to use Evolution with the Microsoft Exchange groupware server that is popular in the corporate world. Although Exchange is an e-mail server, many of its features follow no given standard – instead, they work only with Microsoft's own Outlook groupware program. For Evolution to replace Outlook completely, it had to be able to mimic the non-standard features in Outlook, and Connector was the product Ximian sold to do this. Unlike Evolution, the added features of Connector were not Open Source, but were sold without source code and on licensing terms that allowed only one user per program purchased, as is usual for closed programs.

You'd think their selling a closed program would have caused a protest in the Open Source community, especially as Ximian was one of the best-known proponents of the Free Software ideology. But it never happened. Connector received only positive publicity, presumably because Connector was aimed at existing Microsoft clients and therefore posed no threat to the Linux world. No true supporter of Free Software would ever have owned the Microsoft Exchange server and therefore would have no need for Connector, which made the entire product irrelevant to them. And for any company using Exchange and other Microsoft products it was perfectly normal to pay for a closed Connector – just as they had already paid for Exchange.

Because the sales figures weren't made public, we may never know how well Ximian did out of its Connector product, but according to the company's own statements it did make some money on it. But offhand, it must surely be a fairly marginal product, because any company that wanted to move from Windows to Linux would be more likely to get rid of the Exchange server at the same time. And Connector is useless for anyone using an e-mail server running on Linux, because the free Evolution program is all they'd need. At best, that would have left as potential

---

34   In fact, several e-mail programs were available for Linux before the advent of Evolution, such as Kmail for the KDE desktop environment, and Netscape which many Windows users knew as well. What the people behind Evolution mean by telling the story this way is that there was no e-mail program for the GNOME environment. Another lack that Evolution actually fixed was that at the time there was no groupware solution similar to Microsoft Outlook available for Linux, so no program combined e-mail with calendar and contacts functions.

Connector clients those Linux users who are in a minority at their workplace where most of their colleagues are using Windows and Exchange.

But even so, the Connector episode is an interesting example of the Free Software camp happily accepting, against all their fine principles, the sale of a program, albeit a marginal one, in closed form.

CodeWeavers and **Transgaming Technologies** are two other companies which could be categorised as *playing for both teams*. Both have built their products on top of the Open Source Wine library. The Wine project aims to create a Windows-compatible Linux environment, so that programs made for Windows can be used as such on Linux machines. The task has proved surprisingly difficult and after more than ten years the project is still only in its development stage.

However, CodeWeavers and Transgaming have found Wine is already quite useful within an appropriately limited field. So, with a little extra effort, CodeWeavers made Wine into the product CrossOver Office, which makes it possible to use Microsoft Office on a Linux machine.[35] And Transgaming have found a niche for their product Cedega among game fanatics who want to play their favourite Windows games on their favourite operating system, Linux.

Having finally harnessed Wine for something useful in their respective fields, these two companies are among today's most important contributors to the Wine project. The work they've done is a significant part of the collaborative effort of the entire Wine process, which makes both companies valued members of the Open Source community.

However, their products CrossOver and Cedega are closed programs and, as with Ximian Connector, their target group is not bothered by that. Clients who need to use Microsoft Office or some game from the Windows world aren't going to start complaining about CrossOver or Cedega being closed programs. It simply wouldn't make sense, as their need for Wine is born out of their wanting to use other closed programs.

The staunchest proponents of the Free Software ideology won't bother with too much bashing of companies that, after all, hand over some of the fruits of their labour for the benefit of other Wine users. They are just as unlikely to buy these closed programs but they're satisfied with a silent

---

35 It is also possible to use Lotus Notes, Internet Explorer and some other widespread Windows programs.

boycott. This is noteworthy in a community that is sometimes very loud in its proclamation of the 'right opinion'.

Both CrossOver Office and Cedega have proved to be viable solutions and no doubt there are some customers for them. Again, there are no exact figures, but unlike Ximian Connector, CrossOver and Cedega are the main product of each company. Sales must have been at least reasonable, as both companies still exist.

Verdict: Connector cannot have been an important source of income for Ximian, but it is nonetheless a source of revenue. On the other hand, CrossOver and Cedega are each the mainstay of the company that sells them. So, to some extent, *playing for both teams* does at least work. Significant in these examples is that a Linux company can deviate from the key principle of the Open Source community and sell programs without the source code, i.e. with a closed licence, without there being much protest. Those who do this largely avoid criticism because their products are primarily aimed at clients who use Windows rather than at Linux fanatics who live and breathe the Open Source ideology. On the other hand, the Open Source camp is satisfied because in one way or another such companies are of use to the Open Source movement. This means they are tolerated as companies that are 'good on average'.

Even so, the *playing-for-both-teams* model obviously does not fulfil the criteria of hacker ethics. Also, it feels weird to think that the main source of income for a Linux company would be Windows users, even though it seems there's always plenty of work for bridge-builders in the IT world just as there is in other areas of life.

The story of a failure (Corel)

Now, to turn the tables on the previous examples, we'll look at Corel, a company from the world of Windows that threw out a feeler into the world of Linux. Corel, which is known for its graphics and office programs in Windows, once made a brief foray into the Linux world. Unfortunately, Corel is the warning example here, because it never really managed to fit in with the Linux crowd. It never really became *one of us*.

In 1999, Corel went out on a limb with its own Linux distribution at the same time as it was launching Linux versions of its popular WordPerfect

Office and CorelDraw software. Because the Linux versions available at the time weren't as user-friendly as they are today, Corel also figured that the average WordPerfect user needed a simpler Linux to run it on, so they decided to develop their own Linux version as well.

Because there was no decent word processing program for Linux at the time – at least not one capable of satisfactorily handling documents generated by Word, Microsoft's word processing software – the Linux community was in the main looking forward to the new WordPerfect, but people also thought there was a market for an easy-to-use Linux.

Corel, however, had an ulterior motive for its Linux adventure. The company had been sidelined in the word-processing business, because Microsoft had successfully leveraged the most out of its monopoly. A couple of years earlier, in an attempt to gain independence from Microsoft, Corel had announced it was moving all its programs onto the Java platform. When Java proved wholly unsuitable for the purpose, they piled up their markers on Linux. Corel was ready to go with any technology that could be used to attack the Microsoft hegemony.[36] And what was at stake in this game? Becoming the next Microsoft. The company wanted to offer people an alternative operating system and have it equipped not only with an alternative office program but also with drawing and image processing software.

In part, Corel did this rather well. The company making the world's most popular graphics program left an indelible mark on the KDE desktop environment, for instance, as the KDE programmers learned to tell the difference between icons created by artists and those created by engineers. If nothing else, at least Corel gave Linux a snappy look. In addition to KDE, Corel also put a lot of effort into the Wine project, which it used to port WordPerfect and CorelDraw to Linux.

However, when it was released, the Corel Linux OS was no earth-shattering improvement. Finnish users were surprised to find the operating system offered imperfect support for Scandinavian characters, something other Linux distributions had perfected years ago (naturally enough, since Linux was born in Finland). Although the effort to create expressive

---

36 This is a good contrast to the section on Tolerance in the Part Two of this book, where Linus Torvalds said he wasn't really interested in what Microsoft was doing because he doesn't use Windows. What he did with Linux was to amuse himself. Perhaps Corel ought to have focused more on minding its own business instead of almost bankrupting itself by attacking Microsoft.

graphics and a user-friendly interface was commendable, the novelty quickly paled because of the failure to handle the basics, which negated the benefits of the new easy-to-use features.

Corel Linux was based on the popular distribution Debian Linux. But in those days Debian offered a total of six CDs packed with various Linux programs, whereas Corel had included only one CD's worth in its distribution. Simple is beautiful and all that, but sooner or later many Debian users who tried Corel naturally felt disappointed when some program they wanted to use wasn't available with Corel. However, there was a solution: Corel Linux was still compatible with the installation packages of programs made for Debian, which meant Corel Linux users could stock up their Linux from Debian's well-filled larder.

However, this convenient solution didn't save Corel in the long run. Many Corel Linux users ended up using Debian, because that's where all the good programs were anyway. Nor did staid old Debian suffer from the other little problems that beset Corel: for instance, the non-English alphabets worked as they should. Not only Debian, but the other old Linux versions also held their ground against Corel. The basics were running smoothly and by then the other distributions had also improved their user-friendliness. Finally, Corel could no longer compete.

Corel's Linux adventure exemplifies how difficult it is to be the new kid on the block and challenge companies that have been around longer. One year of Linux experience doesn't give even the best minds in a Windows software company the upper hand against gurus who have been in the business for more than five years, often a couple of decades if you include their Unix experience. There wasn't anything seriously wrong with Corel Linux, but neither was there anything amazing about it.

Although the Linux effort of this large and established software company received a lot of publicity, it failed to set off any great migration of Windows users to Linux. When Corel Linux came, Windows users continued using Windows, and Linux users continued using their own brand of Linux. Because of its size, Corel did attract a fair number of people to try its product, but in the history of Linux it is now no more than a note in the margin.

WordPerfect and CorelDraw didn't do well in the world of Linux either. Despite being eagerly awaited – it was the first time any major software familiar from the world of Windows had been released for Linux – in the end both of them stayed firmly on the retailers' shelves. As Windows users, Corel's old customers didn't need the Linux versions; but it probably surprised Corel more that the Linux users weren't interested either. WordPerfect, which supported Word files, met with some success, but otherwise the Corel Linux project was a flop. Typical Linux users considered WordPerfect to be a bad alternative to Microsoft Word. Both were equally closed, so were of no interest to Linux users committed to Open Source. In addition to which, Microsoft Word was – tough but true – many times better than WordPerfect. So, anyone stuck with using closed software in the first place would at least want to use the best there was, and that wasn't WordPerfect.

Within two years, Corel's Linux adventures had come to an end. They were out of money – most of which had been spent earlier on the failed Java experiment. The company desperately tried to fix its deficit by merging with Borland, but at the last minute the owners of Borland realized what was going on and pulled out. With no cash, Corel was hovering on the brink of bankruptcy when Microsoft – in the middle of its monopoly trial – rescued its competitor with a thick wad of notes. Earlier, Microsoft had done the same thing to prevent Apple from going under. Keeping its competitors alive, albeit feeble, allowed Microsoft to prove in court that it was not a monopoly.

As if by chance, all Corel's Linux projects were closed down just weeks after Microsoft had become a partner. Later, the Linux operations were sold to a company called Xandros, which still publishes an easy-to-use Linux distribution. In the past year or so, Xandros has even become quite a respectable player, although it has yet to match the market share of the big Linux distributions.

With the ease of hindsight, Corel's mistakes can be summed up in two main points. First, the company's motives were all wrong. It squandered the last of its money trying to create a weapon against Microsoft, instead of working on ways to keep its own customers happy.

Second, Corel made a miscalculation that resembles Nokia's WAP adventures. Corel seemed to have thought wrapping Linux in a pretty blue box with the Corel logo on it would be enough to get people rushing to the stores to buy it, just because it was there. Obviously, that just doesn't happen, which Nokia and Corel have both now learned to their cost.

Corel was also spurned for not being *one of us*. The engineers at Corel had downloaded parts of Linux from the Internet, worked on them quite nicely, wrapped it all up, and stuck it on the shelf for people to buy. There was never a true meeting between the Linux community which is used to open development, and Corel which is used to working within the company walls. Had there been more interaction and had it come at an earlier stage, some basic problems – such as the need to incorporate a Scandinavian keyboard – could definitely have been avoided. When Corel later completed the German, French and Dutch versions of its Linux, it marketed the distribution as the first multi-lingual Linux OS. That showed gross arrogance towards the other Linux companies and the Linux community, especially as Corel hadn't even made new translations of its own, but had copied the language versions from other existing Linux distributions, mainly Debian.

Many companies smaller than Corel have tried the same thing. 'Hey, let's copy those free Open Source programs from the Internet, put them on CDs, wrap them up, and sell them,' they think. These small companies are rarely even heard of, but Corel was big enough for its adventure to merit some attention. Even so, such an attitude is a sure sign that you're underestimating others. First and foremost, that's not the way to get in with the *in* crowd. And being alone, Corel was weaker than the rest.

For Corel, the foray into Linux was a sad story, but for the principles of Open Source and for Linux users even this sad story is a victory. If it had been a traditional closed software project, it would have quietly disappeared. The project would have been cancelled and the software would have gone with it. But in the world of Open Source, work that has been done never disappears and a client can rest assured that life will continue, even if a distributor goes bankrupt and stops supporting the product you use.

The work Corel put into the Wine project is still part of today's Wine. And with Wine you can still use CorelDraw and WordPerfect on Linux.[37] KDE is not the same as before the Corel visit, either. Gone is the lacklustre engineering style, and instead KDE has become a really artistic desktop environment, which is even being copied by old hands like Apple and Microsoft! Today's KDE is the work of new artists, but Corel's brief

---

37   But it takes a lot more work now than it did when the same programs were available, ready-to-go, direct from Corel.

participation in the project was revolutionary, and although the company stumbled the work itself was not lost.

Verdict: Corel played its Linux game according to the rules of Open Source and hacker ethics. The company genuinely did a lot of good work on its Linux, but the product flopped. Just making something is no guarantee that customers will flock to buy it. And most of all, it's vital to show some respect for any community you want to join.

A penguin, as in the Linux icon, happens to be a herd animal which makes it an appropriate symbol of hacker ideology. Penguins stay warm by huddling together. Corel tried to survive on its own, and its Corel Linux froze to death.

Don't be too greedy (Java, Ghostscript)

One of the lessons learned from Corel's Linux adventure was that the Linux community shunned CorelDraw and WordPerfect because they were closed programs. Linux users had understood and through their own experience seen the benefits of Open Source, and were no longer interested in closed software, whether or not there was a Linux version available. Why go back to the bad old ways when you've just freed yourself of them?

Open Source has posed a new challenge for companies – still the vast majority – that still make and sell closed programs. It is always only a matter of time before a popular closed program will have to compete with an open program. And since closed programs usually can't compete, at least not in price, with any corresponding Open Source software, the advent of an equally good Open Source alternative usually heralds serious discomfort for the makers of the closed program. For instance, the spread of OpenOffice has already set off the beginning of the end for the overly long dominance of Microsoft Office. It's only a matter of time before the computer giants Oracle, IBM and Microsoft will really have to fight to keep their software in corporate server rooms, rather than the evolving MySQL and PostgreSQL – the Open Source databases which already store most of the Internet's web pages. There are also instances where there was never a race to begin with. For example, from day one, the open Apache web server has had more than 50 per cent of the web server market – the closed web servers were never more than a curiosity.

All this begs the question of how long a manufacturer of closed software can expect to be able to sell his product before the creation of a similar Open Source program comes along. Some rules of thumb can be applied to finding the answer.

Obviously, the simpler a program is, the easier it is to create a competitor – either closed or open. In his essay 'The Cathedral and the Bazaar' Eric Raymond offers another seemingly self-evident rule: *the more popular a program, the more likely it is that there will be an Open Source version of it.* And that seems a reasonable principle to go by. The number of users, or clients, traditionally increases competition and brings down prices. This should also hold true when it comes to the creative processes of Open Source software. The more users, the greater the benefit from an Open Source program and the easier it is to find the motivation to write (or have someone else write) the necessary code.

Another interesting rule might be: *too much greed quickly turns on itself.* For instance, the existence of OpenOffice partly accords with Eric Raymond's rule – after all, there is a vast user base for office programs. But the development of OpenOffice has also been speeded up by the fact that Microsoft, with its virtual monopoly on the market, has hiked the price of its Office package so high that it's becoming unreasonable for private individuals and even small companies to pay so much for basic word processing. This created a crying need for an alternative office program.

Java, the programming language born in the Sun laboratory in the early nineties, has a history which again exemplifies the greed theory. Its strength was considered to be the platform independent 'virtual machine model', which allowed the same Java program to run on Windows, on Unix, or on any other operating system that supports Java. This feature came just as it was needed, around 1995, when use of the Internet and the World Wide Web began growing exponentially. Just as html pages could be read by any computer, Java applets (very small applications) could be used on any computer.

Although the use of applets fizzled out after the first flurry of excitement, Java slowly gained ground and is now the most popular programming language in the world.[38] Its platform independence must have

---

38 Most popular, that is, when a project begins from scratch and the programmer is completely free to choose the language.

played a part in that, but it was largely due to the clarity of the language's object programming interface, its simplicity and a certain academic beauty, that Java is used in all universities today.

Naturally, the Java language has also been used to realize a number of Open Source programs. In particular, the Apache Foundation has done well with several applications in the Java world, and they are also used by commercial Java companies. Even so, Java itself – the Java compiler which turns written source code into a computer program and the Java virtual machine that is needed to run the program – does not yet exist in a respectable Open Source version.

In the early days of Java, an Open Source project called Kaffe tried to come up with some competition for Java. Kaffe was always running a little behind Sun's official Java, but often enough was workable. Today, however, Kaffe is lagging far behind the rest of the Java world. In many instances, it's still usable, but it doesn't yet support the Java 2 standard, published five years ago.

Kaffe is just a virtual machine, not a compiler. IBM, on the other hand, has a fairly good Open Source Java compiler called Jikes. Unlike Kaffe, Jikes has kept up with the development of Java quite well. But again, Jikes is only a compiler – it can't run programs. IBM is also working on a Jikes virtual machine but as yet it doesn't quite meet all the requirements, although it can already run some isolated Java 2 applications.

In latter years, the Free Software Foundation has also stuck its spoon in the Java soup, working to create Java support for its venerable GCC (GNU Compiler Collection) compiler, which already supports nearly all other programming languages. This GCJ (GNU Compiler for Java) project is pretty much on the same level as the Jikes virtual machine – nearly, but as yet not quite in working order.

With Java, too, it's only a matter of time before Open Source alternatives replace Sun's *official* Java. Java may face the same fate as programming languages C- and C++, whereas the Free Software Foundation's GCC has long been the standard to which the closed alternatives of commercial players are compared.

However, Sun has managed to buck this trend for nearly ten years. Considering how popular a language Java is among the Open Source crowd, that's no mean feat. You'd have thought the hackers would have created an alternative that fits their ideology far sooner.

In part, the long time span has been due to the difficulty of the task. Writing a programming language compiler is among the most challenging jobs in the field, comparable for instance with writing the Linux kernel or the GCC (which is in fact a compiler). I read somewhere that a professor at the Helsinki University of Technology said that less than one per cent of all the programmers in the world could even attempt such a task at that level. Another problem with replacing Sun's Java is that the compiler also needs to be a virtual machine, and that's another job that is at least as demanding.

Another factor which is bound to have slowed down the creation of an Open Source alternative is that during all these years, Sun has distributed its own Java for free. Java has never been Open Source, but it has always been available for anybody to use for nothing.

This fact reveals an interesting side to the hacker community. Among the hackers there are idealists like Richard Stallman, people who absolutely refuse to use any closed software, but it seems not all hackers are so wholly idealistic. Most of them seem to feel its OK to use some closed software provided a program is cheap enough – or preferably free.

Sun's Java strategy has been aptly criticized for combining the bad sides of both closed and open software. On the one hand, Java develops slowly and suffers from quality problems due to the *closed* model of development; on the other hand, spreading Java for free hardly benefits Sun financially. Nonetheless, Sun's strategy has also, by chance, been very successful. If Sun had taken Java down the Microsoft route and milked it for huge profits, almost overnight they would have had competition – both closed and open. Instead, Sun has managed to maintain a reasonable balance between openness and greed, which is why it has enjoyed such a long period of popularity. Even so, it won't be long before Jikes or GCJ catch up with it. By the time you're reading this, it may already have happened.

Artifex Software uses a similar strategy to Sun, but whereas Sun's tactics were probably born out of a series of coincidences, Artifex uses them very consciously in the distribution of its popular software Ghostscript. This program is used to view, create, handle and print out PostScript and PDF files, and is particularly popular in the Unix world and Open Source community. Ghostscript has long been the only strong competition for Adobe's PS and PDF products.[39]

The two versions of Ghostscript first saw the light of day at the University of Wisconsin: the almost open AFPL Ghostscript and the completely free GPL Ghostscript. AFPL Ghostscript can be downloaded free from the Web, but cannot then be sold on commercially. For commercial purposes, Artifex sells licensed versions of Ghostscript separately and gives the printer and copier maker Xerox as its reference customer. Although AFPL Ghostscript is free, Artifex also distributes a separate GPL version of Ghostscript, which fulfills even the strictest Open Source terms. Each GPL Ghostscript always corresponds to the previous, roughly one-year-old AFPL Ghostscript, which means clients who have paid for the commercial licence always get a bit more than they would get using the older GPL version. By distributing Ghostscript for free and making the older version 100 per cent Open Source, Artifex ensures that not even the toughest Free Software ideologue will be motivated to challenge Ghostscript.

Verdict: In this section we've looked at how various companies selling closed software handle the pressure from Open Source programs. Summing it up, companies clearly operate at various degrees of mean-spiritedness. Most supporters of the Open Source community are willing to accept a *fair compromise* and will use closed software if it's easily available and cheap – at least, it seems nobody is driven to challenge such software. However, it's evident that too much mean-spirited business practice can be self-defeating. So, don't be too greedy!

Freed I: Netscape/Mozilla

Since the rise of Linux, there has been a lot of debate about whether or not the code of closed software ought to be published, in the way that Open Source programs are made freely available. Sometimes their clients will suggest it to a manufacturer of closed software, sometimes the manufacturers themselves become interested in the benefits to be gained

---

39   Adobe has created both the PostScript and PDF standards. Both technologies can be used for electronic distribution of text documents, etc., although PS is actually a printer control language, whereas PDF has become the standard for distribution of paper files in electronic form – for instance, on the Internet.

from openness. In the late nineties, for instance, at the Microsoft monopoly trial in the US some people argued that the makers of Microsoft Office had an unfair advantage because, unlike their competitors, they had access to the source code for the underlying Windows operating system; and it was therefore demanded that the source code for Windows be made public. The Court, however, did not order this to be done.[40] Latterly, however, originally closed programs are being made open, or 'freed', with ever greater frequency, and now we'll take a look at some of those stories.

Netscape, familiar to all web surfers, was the first serious software to go from being a closed development model to being an Open Source project. This historic event in January 1998 played a part in the invention of the term 'Open Source'.[41] It is said that the managers at Netscape had read, among other things, Eric Raymond's 'The Cathedral and the Bazaar' and become convinced that the open development model might save Netscape from doom.

Although in many ways 1998 can be seen as the year in which Linux and the open development model really took off and entered the consciousness of the corporate world – which was much thanks to the process Netscape had begun – Netscape's decision wasn't really such a gift to the Open Source community as one might at first think. Microsoft's Internet Explorer had already taken the leading role in the browser wars and was also ahead of Netscape in quality. Also, Netscape seemed to become weaker with each version that was released. It wasn't long before the announcement that Netscape, the very company that had set off and embodied the Internet boom, had reached the point where it would be divided into parts. By the end of 1998, Sun and AOL had split up the remains between them. AOL took over the browser and the Open Source project called Mozilla. The Netscape company lived on as the greatest legend of the 'new economy', but in reality it was just a shooting star – all but one of the four years of its business, that had promised so much, were in the red. And perhaps that is actually a good summation of the turn of the millennium's 'new economy'.

---

40 Soon after George W. Bush came to power the trial was brought to a speedy end by the Court expediently finding Microsoft guilty of abusing its monopolistic position, but imposing no sanctions.

41 Prior to this, the only term used was 'Free Software'.

After all the initial excitement, the Mozilla project proved, at least in part, to be a disappointment. It soon transpired that in the fight to beat Microsoft, Netscape's programmers had been pressed for time and had produced really confusing and low-quality code. In the first couple of years Mozilla was mostly a clean-up project. Finally, the Mozilla coders came to the conclusion that the easiest thing was really to simply rewrite the key part of the browser, the component that shows www pages. Not until this was done was there any sort of backbone to the project. In the end, Mozilla 1.0 was published four and a half years after the start of the project.

One of the leaders of the Mozilla project, Jamie Zawinski correctly observed that Open Source wasn't just 'magic pixie dust', and he was right. There is no power in the world that can save a programming project that is all spaghetti code, rambling, and all else that is the consequence of less than top-quality programming. Although by now there are several really good versions of Mozilla available, and in particular the number of bugs has decreased dramatically since the days of Netscape, the slowness and its sprawling code was long a topic to which people kept returning. Possibly, it was in part due to a problem in the project's culture. Perhaps it carried a ballast of casual attitude to quality, inherited with the Netscape code.

The Firefox browser was separated from the Mozilla project, but was based on the same original code. However, a different set of people ran the Firefox project. The first official version, Firefox 1.0, was published in November 2004, and finally put an end to the slowness and other inherited problems. Like a phoenix, Firefox had risen from the ashes of old Netscape. Younger, more colourful and supporting a lot of new technologies, Firefox came to challenge the dinosaur Internet Explorer which latterly hadn't been moving forward.

From 1998 to 2004 was a long time in terms of the changes taking place in the IT business. However, we must remember that the Mozilla project had had other important goals – goals that had been reached a lot earlier. Although in the end Microsoft took more than 90 per cent of the browser market – which, at the time of writing, it still holds – the Mozilla project by its mere existence guaranteed that the Web didn't become Microsoft's exclusive property. The existence of more than one browser ensures that home-page makers – at least those who know what they're doing – stick to common standards, which denies Microsoft both complete monopoly and the opportunity to dictate development.

Also, in the shape of Firefox, the Mozilla project finally achieved its proper goal: it became the best browser in the world, better and faster than its competition. If you believe the statistics, Mozilla and Firefox are still marginal in the browser market – though Firefox is steadily climbing the charts – but for the first time in a long while Internet Explorer is lagging behind its three biggest competitors, technically.[42] Although not much is left of the original Netscape browser, there is good reason to be grateful to those who set the Mozilla project in motion. The community that has grown up around Mozilla has proved stronger than the substandard spaghetti code that it inherited. The Mozilla project has given the Open Source community far more than the browser called Mozilla. For instance, the Bugzilla tool, used in almost all Open Source programming projects, is an offshoot of Mozilla, and is also used by many software companies in the production of closed programs.

Finally, it has to be said that an historical wheel has come full circle with Mozilla. The Netscape browser was based on the Mosaic browser originally developed in the academic environment of the National Center for Supercomputing Applications (NCSA).[43] When the code for Netscape was released under the Mozilla project, it can be said to have returned to its roots. And actually Mozilla's Web browser is only part of a bigger story: the World Wide Web technology was originally developed in the CERN laboratory, from which is was given to the world, open and free. And before the Web was invented, the entire Internet and all its technologies and standards had evolved in the same way, in the community of Unix hackers, in accordance with the principles of openness. When open Apache became the most common Web server, closed Netscape was actually a tiny freak in an open world – which makes Mozilla the prodigal son returned.

Verdict: The opening of the Netscape code began the popularizing of the Open Source movement, making it a viable alternative for other companies too. Open Source was a kind of defence mechanism for Netscape, for it to make a stand against Microsoft's crushing ascendancy, and in that the strategy worked. Technically, however, the Mozilla project faced enormous challenges. Many years of uncontrolled growth of spaghetti code and the

---

42 In addition to the Mozilla family (Mozilla and its derivatives Netscape, Firefox, Galeon, etc.), Internet Explorer has two other competitors in the closed Opera and the open Konqueror, which is also the basis for Apple's new browser Safari.

43 The same is true for the closed Internet Explorer.

problems that caused didn't magically evaporate under the influence of openness – sorting out the problems took much longer than anyone could have foreseen.

Freed II: InterBase/Firebird

Borland became known for its good programming tools in the nineties. In fact, I wrote my very first Java application using Borland's JBuilder which came on a free CD. For reasons nobody as yet seems to understand, this well-known company had some sort of identity crisis at the end of the nineties. In a misguided effort to create a brand name, the company renamed itself Inprise. As it soon became apparent that nobody had ever heard of the company called Inprise and that everybody went on calling Borland *Borland*, the management then changed the name to Inprise/Borland.com, and soon after that to Borland/Inprise, and finally back to the familiar Borland.[44] Of all the crazy IT stories from the turn of the millennium, the Borland-Inprise-Borland one takes the prize for most schizophrenia.

One of Borland's products, which it had purchased in 1991, was the SQL database called InterBase.[45] Although not on a level with its bigger cousins Oracle and IBM DB2, InterBase was fairly common for smaller database use.

Just before the end of December 1999, the professional and determined leaders of Borland – actually, *Inprise* at the time – announced to the developers of InterBase that they were halting the development of the database. Apparently, the management was unhappy with the level of profit InterBase was generating. Even though the product was not in the red, for some reason they'd decided to pull the plug on it.

Borland's customers weren't happy. Big clients like Nokia and Motorola used InterBase widely and in important projects, and if nothing else helped they were even prepared to buy the whole InterBase division from Borland. With big clients like that putting pressure on Borland, the company finally compromised by deciding to release InterBase under an Open Source licence.

---

44 At this point I'm sure one is allowed a smile. Earlier in this book I've spoken against planning and predetermination, but you have to draw the limit somewhere!

45 InterBase itself had been created way back in 1984.

And that, one would think, was that. But not a bit of it, the story is just begun.

When the Borland management finally cottoned on to how strong a product they had, they suddenly changed their minds. Of course they ought to go on *selling* such a good product – what with big clients coming with bags of money and practically begging them to do so. So when the first Open Source version, InterBase 6.0, was released, Borland started pulling out of the project. Suddenly, the company gave the Open Source version no guarantee or support, and on the whole the company went back to the good old way of closed software, charging their clients according to the one license per machine principle.

The result of this confusing and partly amusing story was Firebird, the genuinely *open* Open Source version of InterBase. The Firebird project amassed a number of programmers who were fed up with the yo-yoing at Borland and were determined to keep working on the open version on their own. Borland's own programmers weren't involved in Firebird, but it was developed by some accomplished programmers from outside Borland who had worked on the first versions of InterBase back in the eighties, together with some other programmers and consultants who had worked with InterBase.

In many ways the first years of Firebird resembled the tale of Mozilla. When the code of a closed program is opened up, all the garbage that has been quietly swept under the carpet over a period of years is suddenly revealed. It is said that one of the first surprises was that compiling the InterBase code into runnable program code produced several thousand warnings of possible flaws in the code. Such 'compiler warnings' don't necessarily signify serious problems and don't usually prevent a program from working, but the fact that there were thousands of them says something about the attitude of the programmers working on InterBase.

When a program is developed openly, the situation usually never gets as bad as it was with InterBase and Mozilla. In the development of closed programs, there is always the temptation to take the line of least resistance. Flaws are unimportant: if the program runs and functions and seems superficially OK, it's put on the market right away. The quality of an Open Source program is open for all to see, not to mention the personal reputation of the writers of the code being at stake; so, working in an open environment raises the bar.

The Firebird hackers had to spend the first year or so cleaning up the code. And that long overdue spring cleaning certainly revealed some hairy skeletons in the InterBase cupboard.

In InterBase, as in database products in general, it is possible to define a number of different user IDs and give these users different rights. The person in charge of the database can have the right to do anything, a secretary can have the right to add or delete data, while other users only have the right to read but not change the data. User IDs, passwords, and the level of each user's rights must, of course, be stored in a way that allows the database program to access the information.

In the case of database software, the programmer is lucky in that a database is just the place to store user information. That's how InterBase had done it. The trouble with such an arrangement is that it leads to a chicken-or-egg situation. For a user to access the database, the user ID and password must first be checked, *but* the user ID and password are stored within the database that can't be accessed until the user ID and password have been checked!

There are probably a number of ways to get around this problem, but in 1992 the Borland programmers chose a solution that must be the most direct. They added a so-called hard-coded extra user ID and password giving access to all databases within InterBase! This user ID had been used internally within the InterBase code to bypass the chicken-or-egg problem, i.e., to check if the user ID and password given were correct. But once the code had been made open and the password that bypassed all further checks was there for all to read, it could also be used to break into anybody's database.[46]

Another skeleton in the InterBase cupboard was almost as bad. To ease their testing, the Borland quality control unit had demanded that the program contained a command that would allow a database to be scrambled or completely destroyed.[47] Inexplicably, they insisted that this command be left in the version of InterBase that was sold to customers. Obviously, the

---

[46] You must note that the openness of the code was not the problem, but the laziness and irresponsibility of the original Borland engineer. The code would have been easy to spot even before the Open Source release of InterBase; all you had to do was to look at InterBase's machine code files with an ordinary text editor. It is perfectly possible that some cracker did this – the 'back door' had been in existence for nearly ten years.

[47] Most likely the command was used to create artificial error situations to test how the software handles them.

InterBase user manual contained no information about this command, which was only intended for internal use by the quality control department, but leaving a destroy-all-files type of command in a version to be sold to clients does sound a bit like playing Russian roulette with their data. Even more incredible is that this was apparently done at the express request of the quality control department.

So, how have things been with the Firebird project since then?

It's doing fine, thank you very much. It took a little over a year to sort out the worst messes, then it was another six months before Firebird 1.0 was published in March 2002. Though the Firebird hackers got through their spring cleaning sooner than their comrades cleaning up the Mozilla code, this too shows what an enormous job it is to inherit the responsibility of developing an old program.

Firebird has done reasonably well, but it hasn't had the same reception in the Open Source community as Mozilla, because the open MySQL and PostgreSQL already more than adequately satisfy the hacker community's need for databases. Firebird has, instead, found its customers among the old InterBase users, who no longer need to be that worried about Borland's quirks.

Verdict: The InterBase story clearly exemplifies the risks involved in using closed programs. What are customers to do when a manufacturer decides to stop developing a product they really, really need? Building the IT infrastructure of a company on Open Source programs is always a safer option, because it allows the user of a program to make their own decisions about the future. As was the case with Mozilla, the first year of Firebird exposed how much can be hidden or overlooked within a closed program, while revealing how much better the quality of an open program is likely to be. It has been said the security of Open Source programs is better, because openness helps reveal the bugs in a code. In the case of Firebird, this did happen, but it actually took more than six months before a critical gap in the defences was found – despite the fact that it was obvious and easily identifiable in the code.

Freed III: Quake

id Software will go down in history as the company that published the first three-dimensional shooting game for PCs. You probably haven't heard of

Hovertank 3D – I certainly hadn't – but its successors are legendary: *Quake* and *Doom*. *Quake*, which you could play over the Internet, had a particularly loyal fan base. For them, apparently, nothing was more fun than crawling around a sewerage system using a flame-thrower to shoot at friends dressed up as bogey-men – virtually, that is.

The man behind these games, John Carmack, decided to give all *Quake* fans a special gift for Christmas 1999. He used an Open Source licence to publish the source code for *Quake 1* on the Internet. This was no great sacrifice: the sales of the game had already dwindled to next to nothing, and id Software was selling several new games, fancier than the first, among them *Quake 2* and *Quake 3*, and their code was not made public.

However, soon after the happy surprise, chaos reigned in the world of *Quake*. The publication of the source code had led to cheating in multiplayer Internet games! Skilful programmers made changes in their own *Quake*, enabling their characters to automatically dodge all bullets coming their way.[48] Or they programmed their character to aim at and shoot all enemies as soon as they appeared – and to do so at lightning speed. Another good scam was to program all walls in the game to be transparent, which allowed the player to see enemies hiding around corners, while the enemies played the game in a version with solid walls.

Although the programming of such X-ray vision and automatic ducking can be an interesting challenge in itself – a challenge programmers could compete in, actually – many *Quake* players were irritated by the cheating versions of the game. It's not much fun playing against someone who is impossible to hit and who can see through walls.

Eric Raymond, always keen to promote the Open Source idea, hurried to publish an essay on this fascinating problem. He suggested that it was yet another example of how easy it was for closed programs to go for solutions that aren't really safe and which can't take open scrutiny. He argued that if *Quake* had been created in an open model from the start, such problems would have been dealt with at an early stage and therefore avoided.

In this, however, Eric was wrong! The problems with *Quake* had nothing to do with its creators sitting in their closed world and choosing shortcuts that compromised security. In fact, you couldn't cheat by giving yourself an unending supply of weapons and ammunition, for instance,

---

48 I can't help thinking that the *Matrix* scriptwriters must have played this version of *Quake*!

because such things had been made impossible at the designing stage of the game. The nature of all the methods of cheating (except the X-ray vision) was that the player had used his own computer as an aid to play better, be it for better aim or something else. This way of cheating could theoretically have been realized earlier, without access to the source code, but publication of the code made it a lot easier and perhaps also more fun.

Actually, the problem highlighted by the cheating in *Quake* had been realized earlier elsewhere. Playing postal chess had long ago been ruined by chess computer games. The mere suspicion that your opponent might be using the help of a computer was enough to spoil the fun. This is why postal chess is so rare today.

Learning more about the nature of, and reasons for, the cheating also led to the understanding that this was a problem particular to games. In real life we use computers to help us with difficult tasks; that's the whole point of having one. In the military, computers are used to improve aim – just as those who cheated in *Quake* had done – and nobody thinks that's unfair. Or if we go for a more peaceful example, nobody would accuse me of cheating when I use a computer program to find the cheapest of whatever I want to buy from all that is offered on eBay. That is precisely what computers were invented to do!

But the world of games is different. The idea of a game is that everybody plays it by the same rules, without supplementary technical aids. If I wanted to travel a distance of 26 miles (42 km) as quickly as possible, I'd go by car, or perhaps by helicopter. But if it's a marathon race, it would obviously be cheating to go by car.

Not only would it be cheating, it would be boring. And that's what the *Quake* players concluded. Cheating is boring. It takes all the excitement out of the game. One player got it right when he said: 'I play *Quake* like I play any other game. Only with friends – who don't cheat.'

Verdict: The story of cheaters in *Quake* is interesting because the Open Source model creates problems that would never arise with a closed program. However, the problem is limited to Internet gaming, or perhaps rather to 'remote game playing', such as postal chess. In the 'real world' the Open Source model still seems to lead to better security. Finally, it has to be said that there are a lot of multiplayer Internet games with accessible source code, just as there are probably still those who play postal chess.[49]

From the above it is clear that opening up the source code of a program that has been developed in closed circumstances isn't as rosy a prospect as might be supposed. The code in many closed programs is often so abysmal it doesn't bear exposure. There are often horrible skeletons in the closet. In the case of *Quake*, the Open Source model led to totally unexpected problems, a situation nobody foresaw.

These stories throw new light on the demands to open up the source code of Windows, for instance. Who knows what skeletons you might find there? In the monopoly trial, Microsoft defended itself against demands to open up the code by saying that it would constitute a threat to US national security to publicize it. The Open Source people laughed to hear Microsoft say this. 'That's what we've been saying all along, that a buggy Windows is a threat to the security of us all!' But having learnt from the stories of Mozilla, Firebird, and *Quake*, it is right to take the Microsoft claim seriously. In short, security concerns suggest it would be best not to use closed programs, but now that we are using them it's probably better to keep them closed.[50] Mozilla, InterBase, and *Quake* each represent a slightly different philosophy about why it was worth making the code public.

The managers at Netscape decided to open up the source code for Mozilla as a sort of defence. As an Open Source project Mozilla has achieved what Netscape couldn't make happen with a closed program. Even Microsoft couldn't crush the open code. The code was opened at the last minute, however; Mozilla was saved, but for Netscape the company it was too late.

---

49 One of the most popular Open Source shooting games is *BZFlag* which can be played on Windows, Mac and Linux as well as other variations of Unix. http://BZFlag.org/

50 On February 12, 2004 a large portion of the Windows source code leaked on to the Internet due to security problems at a Microsoft partner (http://slashdot.org/articles/04/02/13/165231.shtml). We are therefore facing the worst possible situation *vis-à-vis* Windows: it has been developed as a closed program, which means it has more inherent security risks than for instance Linux. The code has leaked into the public domain, which means crackers have an easy time looking for the flaws. At the same time, programmers who might be able to help Microsoft find the problems and fix them cannot do so because it is illegal to be in possession of the code. Microsoft is therefore threatened by all the dangers associated with a sudden publication of closed code without being able to take advantage of the positive aspects of the Open Source process.

In the case of InterBase, it was the clients using the product who were looking for shelter. The decision to stop developing a closed program is always a threat to its users. Whereas, users of open programs are free of such threats.

With *Quake*, it wasn't about anyone protecting themselves, but rather more of a cultural achievement. Since *Quake*, many other games have been 'set free'. Their source codes give the fans pleasure, even though the financial heyday of the game was over long ago. Many games can be ported to new platforms, for instance, if the source code is available. Old Windows games are finding new life on Linux machines, or you can play an old Commodore 64 game on Windows. So, Open Source is also about preserving our heritage!

Freed IV: StarOffice/OpenOffice.org

The biggest problem for Linux users and would-be Linux users throughout the nineties was the lack of proper office software. Actually, I don't think there was a good alternative for any Unix-type operating system. Scientists at universities would have written their articles 'in code' with LaTeX or HTML using, for instance, Emacs, the venerable text editing software created by Richard Stallman. But even most scientists would probably have done what everyone else did: they used Windows together with either Microsoft or Corel office applications. The lack of an office program – and particularly the lack of word-processing software – was often a crucial hindrance to anyone wanting to move from Windows to Linux.

To rectify this, there were naturally some Open Source projects. AbiWord and Kword are popular word processing programs, while Gnumeric and Kspread replace the spreadsheet program Excel and KPresenter replaces PowerPoint. However, to replace the whole of Microsoft Office is not easy, and to be honest even today, in 2004, none of these projects are on a level where they could seriously challenge MS Office.

The problem is not that one couldn't write a text using these programs; it's that they don't do well enough in reading Microsoft Word documents. In an era when a lot of files are sent attached to e-mail, it's imperative that files generated by monopolistic Microsoft can be opened flawlessly. Because these file formats are not public standards, it's not all that easy to write a competitive program – in fact, it requires a lot of guesswork, trial and error.

Closed software was slightly better at overcoming the same problem. Applix was a popular package of office programs and it used to come with a lot of Linuxes. Corel's WordPerfect made its short Linux visit before Corel dropped out of the Linux experiment and left the WordPerfect users on Linux empty-handed.

StarOffice, from the German company StarDivision, was also very popular. This software's popularity was increased by it being free to private users. In addition to which, it could be run on both Linux and Windows. Even so, StarOffice has never been as popular as WordPerfect or Word, but it has nonetheless had a relatively long and distinguished history since its first versions were developed back in the days of DOS.

In August 1999, Sun announced that it had bought StarDivision and with it the StarOffice software. Sun also let it be known that it had plans to publish the StarOffice code under an Open Source licence. Because StarOffice was already a popular office software among Linux users, this news was greeted with jubilation.

Sun handled the Open Source release of StarOffice a lot better than Netscape and Borland did theirs. It took nearly a year before any code was actually published. During that time the code was cleaned up and some of the German documentation was translated into English, so that as many hackers as possible would be able to understand the open code. Some time was also spent on removing code that wasn't Sun's to open, i.e. where the copyright was owned by third parties and therefore couldn't be published under an Open Source licence. In the end, the code was released in July 2000. In October the OpenOffice.org website followed, becoming the home of the hacker community developing the code as well as the name of the Open Source version of the software.[51]

StarOffice was no dream gift for the hacker community – in quality, it was comparable to InterBase and Netscape. One of the most immediately visible quirks was that in StarOffice all the programs, from word processing

---

51 Sun still also sells an office program under the name of StarOffice. It is nearly identical to OpenOffice, but also includes some non-open extensions, such as fonts and an Access-type database program.
The official name of OpenOffice is 'OpenOffice.org' (OOo, for short), because plain 'OpenOffice' was already a registered trademark. Unofficially, the name used is practically without exception OpenOffice.

and spreadsheets to its e-mail program and browser, were one and the same program. And in order to make the program look the same on all operating systems, whether for use on a Linux or a Windows machine, there was a user interface that replaced the real operating system, from the *Start* button to file management. The idea must have been to ease the difficulties arising from the differences between the operating systems, but for most people the result was pretty much the opposite. StarOffice seemed equally weird to both Windows and Linux users.

So to begin with, OpenOffice was also mainly a clean-up project. The cleaners chose to get rid of the browser and e-mail program altogether because there were better Open Source alternatives. The single chunk of office software was chopped up into separate programs for word processing, spreadsheets, and so on. Sun's careful preparation and commitment to the project together with the enormous interest in the 'missing link' of Open Source applications helped the clean-up crew over the first hurdles. Only a year after the OpenOffice.org project was founded they were able to release the Build 638c version, which was a relatively stable and usable test version of the new open office software. OpenOffice 1.0 was published on May Day 2002. By then, more than six million copies of trial versions like Build 638c had been downloaded from the website.

For a long time now, Linux has been a good choice for a server operating system, but in the nineties it had yet to become a serious contender for desktop computing. OpenOffice has changed all that. Even before the final 1.0 version many cities and nation states started finding out how it might be possible to switch to Linux and OpenOffice in their offices. Many German cities, Munich was the first of them, have made this decision. In the corporate world Novell, for one, has found that as the largest Linux company, it actually has a responsibility to show the way, so it too intends to give up using Microsoft software as soon as possible.

The move away from the Microsoft monopoly to the open world is eased by both Mozilla and OpenOffice being compatible with Windows, which eases the changeover. First, while still running a computer on Windows, one starts using the open software browser, e-mail, word processing and spreadsheets.[52] After this it's time to start switching from Windows to Linux, and users hardly notice the difference as they continue to use the

---

52 Mozilla also has an e-mail program. There are many other e-mail programs for Linux, and Mozilla is not the most popular of them but it is the only one that will run on both Windows and Linux.

same software programs. Novell, for instance, will make the changeover in this way. You too can take the first step towards more open data processing right now. And installing Mozilla and OpenOffice on your computer won't even cost anything!

The advent of OpenOffice was a key step forwards in enabling the use of Linux on desktop computers, but there remains the question: what did Sun get out of all of this? Was the purchase of StarDivision only charity, or was it more about buying a stick to poke at Sun's archenemy, Microsoft?

It wasn't charity, but Sun's relationship to Microsoft may have played a part. Sun's relationship with Linux has been difficult. Linux is strong competition for Solaris, Sun's own operating system, and keeps gobbling up ever larger slices of the Solaris market. Which is why Sun has seen Linux as a threat, and some of the craziest things CEO Scott McNealy has said about Linux can actually hold a flag to Bill Gates' infamous statement about Linux being a Communist and anti-American system.

In desktop software, the opposite is the case, because in that area Linux and Solaris are both underdog competitors to Microsoft. The desktop software for Solaris is mostly copied from Linux GNOME, but it was still short of an office software bundle. Sun donated StarOffice to the Open Source movement, because it was obvious that the open development model was their only chance of challenging Microsoft.

I don't know if Sun's attitude of 'your worst enemy is also your best ally' is a sign of schizophrenia or if it's just post-modern, but in any case OpenOffice has been a success – also from Sun's point of view. Sun has sold its own StarOffice version in the millions – although most were sold very cheap, for instance to universities. At the end of 2003 Sun came out with a news bombshell; it had made a deal with the People's Republic of China to sell up to 200 million Linuxes for desktop use at $50 a pop. The existence of OpenOffice, along with Mozilla and many other Linux desktop programs, were a requirement for a deal like this and they are of course included in the package. After the deal with China the company has done a lot more Linux business around the world with, for instance, demand rising for Sun Linux desktops in the UK.

Verdict: OpenOffice is arguably the most successful and definitely most important project in which a closed old program has been released under an Open Source licence. The release of OpenOffice 1.0 removed the last barrier for far-reaching Linux planning in companies and the public services.

Furthermore, it seems that the OpenOffice venture will prove to be a financially successful investment for Sun.

Freed V: Eclipse

On 5 November 2001, IBM sent out a press release announcing a donation of $40 million worth of tools to the Open Source community. The press release made it clear that this was all about some sort of application used for Java programming, but in real life most of the hacker community, or the IT business at large, had never heard of IBM's Eclipse.

A number of reasonably good programming environments already existed for the Java market, and IBM had realized that this made its own Java programming environment – at that point not yet called Eclipse – a less than sensible investment. Not that there was anything particularly wrong with the IBM toolset, but nor was it significantly ahead of its competition either. Which meant it would probably never replace the competition. Indeed, there was a risk that things would go the other way and IBM's offering would be superseded by a competitor's product.

However, IBM didn't want to give up its programming tool, as it was an irreplaceable part of the IBM portfolio – its main products being an expensive Unix and Linux server, the DB2 database and the Websphere Java application server. It would be hard to sell clients an application server if at the same time there wasn't also a tool for programming the application components for the server. Getting the programming tool from a third party – such as Sun or Borland – didn't appeal to IBM. That would mean spending money outside the company; and also, IBM wouldn't want to end up being way too dependent upon the unpredictable quirks of companies like Borland-Inprise-Inprise/Borland-Borland/Inprise-Borland.

In other words, an interesting situation. IBM had to keep developing Eclipse; yet, financially, investing in it was a bad idea. The solution, of course, was Open Source.

IBM had already grasped the idea of Linux and Open Source before they released Eclipse. While many other businesses in the IT sector saw the distribution of programs for free as a dire threat to their own existence, IBM had understood that even when people had switched to Linux there would still be plenty of work for IBM to do. In fact, IBM already had experience of

Linux, and that experience had shown them that clients bought as many IBM servers as ever and paid just as much for them, even when they ran on Linux. In fact, now that the IBM servers were running on Linux, even more people were buying them. The only difference to the old Unix servers was that the development of Linux didn't rest solely on IBM. In other words, labour costs went down while revenue went up!

As news of Eclipse, and knowledge of what it really was, spread it gathered more developers and a lot of users. Today, it can be described as the best and most popular Java development environment available. Which means it very quickly became a success story; much faster than, say, OpenOffice or Mozilla. In addition to Java, it now has modules for C- and C++ programming, as well as many other uses, such as programming in Python. Once again, the Open Source development model has shown its strength and wealth and outperformed all competitors.

Where OpenOffice satisfied a need in the Linux world, the situation was different with Eclipse. There was no lack of Java programming tools – in fact, there were too many of them! They were all reasonably good, but none of them came close to the brilliance of today's Eclipse. The existence of so many different tools was a problem for all companies working in the Java market, as the programs did not follow any agreed standard and caused unnecessary training costs, etc. When all parties gathered around one common and open solution, less effort quickly gave better results.

Before Eclipse, most Open Source projects had been collaborations which centred around a single private individual – such as Linus Torvalds – or were administered by non-profit umbrella organizations founded by individuals – like the Apache Software Foundation. Mozilla and OpenOffice were still administered by their old parent companies, but they weren't collaborations between companies, as the participants were mostly individual programmers. IBM, however, had gathered an impressive group of 150 collaborating companies behind Eclipse, and their first press release mentioned in particular Red Hat, Rational and TogetherSoft. Soon more businesses joined, among them Oracle and Borland. It's encouraging to see that businesses can actually be successfully involved in Open Source projects at an organizational level.

Verdict: The incomplete Eclipse was dropped into the lap of the Open Source community like a bolt from the blue and quickly became a very functional and versatile Java programming tool which outperformed its

116

numerous competitors. IBM is the one old IT business that has adopted the rules of the Open Source world better than the rest, which is why Big Blue is doing swimmingly alongside the Linux penguin.

Freed VI: Blender

Blender, which makes 3D animations, started in 1995 as an internal programming project in the Dutch animation studio NeoGeo. It replaced the animation program previously used by NeoGeo, which originally had also been developed for internal use.

The average computer user sees Microsoft and other manufacturers of finished programs as the embodiment of software production, but in reality most of the worlds' programmers work on internal programs for specific companies, such as Blender. Programmers work everywhere and anywhere, from banks and insurance companies to film studios, because the programs needed by such businesses aren't always available 'off the peg'.

Because Blender was such a brilliant program, its creator Ton Roosendaal decided to externalize the development of it to a separate company called Not a Number. The idea was for NaN to sell licences to Blender for other animation studios to use and get revenue from the consultation services surrounding it. The new Blender software was presented at the Siggraph animation conference, where it immediately awakened a lot of interest. The company was then able to raise a total of €4.5 million from venture capitalists and soon had 50 full-time programmers working on Blender. The first version – known as version 2.0 – was released in the summer of 2000 and by the end of the year Blender had 250,000 registered users.

Unfortunately, something went wrong and the capital was spent before the project was properly up and running. In April, new investors had put their weight behind Blender and the development was continued by a reborn but considerably smaller NaN. Six months later this new NaN company released Blender Publisher, which was designed to do the *in* thing, i.e., create three-dimensional interactive media on the Web. However, the sales figures for the product were a disappointment and the second lot of investors also decided to pull out. The company quit all operations and development of Blender was discontinued.

Although Blender hadn't conquered the world, it already had a loyal user base. Encouraged by the feedback from these users, Ton Roosendaal tried a third time to save Blender, and this rescue operation did work.

Ton founded the Blender Foundation and made a deal with the investors who owned the rights to Blender. The investors agreed to sell Blender to the Foundation for €100,000 under the GPL licence, thus enabling the Foundation to keep developing the software according to the principles of Open Source.

For venture capitalists who have lost several million, the offer of €100,000 is naturally better than nothing. And the deal didn't involve Ton in any risk either – but how would he raise the €100,000?

To his own surprise and that of all the other people who had been involved in Blender, Ton and the other former employees of NaN managed to raise the money in a mere seven weeks! On Sunday 13 October, 2002, Blender was turned over, under GPL licence, to the caring hands of the Open Source community.

As an Open Source program, Blender once more came to life. There have already been several new versions. The number of users is increasing and a whole community is growing up around the software. Thousands of users chat on Blender's website and on IRC. Images and short films made using Blender can be viewed, and admired, via the many links on the Blender website. The program can also be used to make games and some Open Source games have already been built around the software's games engine.

Financially, the makers of Blender have also moved from the traditional venture capitalist model to Open Source financing. For the Blender Foundation's fundraiser in 2003, some 3,000 copies of the new Blender guide were sold. At the beginning of 2004 the Foundation received research and development grants from the EU to the tune of €140,000. Thanks to this funding, both large and small, together with numerous hackers volunteering for the project, Blender's future looks brighter than ever.

Verdict: Through citing several examples, this section of the book has considered whether or not it is possible to build a viable business on the Open Source development model. Despite the number of examples, you may remain not yet wholly convinced; or perhaps you're thinking that, along with the closed development model, Open Source may be a model that is 'OK', a model that 'does work'. However, the story of Blender turns the tables on that question. What is wrong with the closed and venture capitalism based 'traditional' programming development, which twice failed with Blender and nearly killed off a great product? After all, this product had a brilliant future ahead of it – but not until the right business model was found!

End of the road, the journey begins (*Linux Weekly News*)

'The end of the road', read the surprising headline on the front page of the *Linux Weekly News* (LWN) of 24 July, 2002.[53] Founded in 1998, it had established itself as the most reliable, expert, and analytical Web publication of the Linux community. Today, *Linux Weekly News*, like *Linux Today* and *Slashdot*, publishes daily links to various Linux news sites, but its mainstay was always a weekly issue consisting of original articles.

As usual, in the last July issue it published articles relating to the world of Open Source, and included stories on: RealNetworks' decision to switch to the Open Source development model; US plans for legislation that would give film studios and record companies the right to harass and possibly break into the computers of Internet users of their choice without any police or court order; security problems at PHP and SSH; the cli() and sti() functions of the Linux kernel, and the publication of Ogg Vorbis 1.0 and Debian GNU/Linux 3.0. Then, out of the blue, at the end of the main page was an article under the heading 'The End of the Road'.

Linux Weekly News had come to the conclusion that banner advertising wasn't a viable way of financing a free webzine.[54] For some time, LWN accepted donations from its readers through the PayPal system, and even though the income generated was somewhat bigger than the advertising revenue, it still wasn't enough to finance a staff of five. Having considered the option of making LWN a subscription webzine, the people behind LWN finally decided to call it a day. The issue of 1 August, 2002, would be the last. There was nothing else to be done; the decision was final.

---

53   http://lwn.net

54   This may not sound like a very surprising conclusion, but in the golden nineties even banner advertising seemed like a smart idea.

The reaction of LWN readers to this announcement surprised everybody, including its editors and the readers themselves.[55] Naturally, the demise of the most esteemed journalistic publication focusing on Linux caused great disappointment, even shock, but the response to the announcement being what it was, on a practical level, was historic.

> Posted Jul 25, 2002 20:26 UTC (Thu) by other-iain
> I've read LWN for about 4 years. My guess is that a reasonable subscription price would have been $30 a year. That's $120. I gave $20 earlier, so that leaves $100 unpaid. I've just put that $100 in through PayPal. Consider this payment for services rendered. I'm sorry to see you go, but I understand why [...]
>
> Good luck in your post-LWN ventures. Let us know who you're writing for next so we can tune in.

> Posted Jul 26, 2002 0:46 UTC (Fri) by BogusUser
> I did the same, registered to donate, and to say thanks for the great work over the years. If these extra donations do not make enuf of a difference I smile thinking of you having a beer on me.

> Posted Jul 26, 2002 14:19 UTC (Fri) by jgm
> I hope you find your miracle. I've donated my US$100. I hope it helps keep you going. If not, consider it my late :-(subscription fee for your fine publication.
>
> I've found LWN to be the best site for keeping up with what is happening in the GNU/Linux, Free Software, and Open Source Software world. I'm really going to miss you!! I especially enjoyed the Kernel section. My Thursday's are just not going to be the same without LWN!
>
> In any case, best of luck to you all and thanks for the great work you've done on LWN. I hope you can find a way to continue.

By the time the following week's issue was published, a total of $25,000 had been donated! For a staff of five editors, that would only cover expenses for about six weeks, but it did make the LWN staff rethink their decision to close LWN down. After a week-long break, they decided to turn LWN into a subscription webzine. The daily newslinks and the accompanying user

---

55   Readers' reactions are still available in the comments to the article at
     http://lwn.net/Articles/5409/

forums would remain open to all, but the weekly publication of original articles would be available to subscribers only, and the price was set at $5 a month. However, LWN's loathing for the closed model proved so strong that the staff decided that all articles over a week old would be made available to non-subscribers.

After this decision, although LWN had to slightly reduce the number of permanent contributors and partly make do with freelance writers, life went on virtually unchanged. In 2003, LWN showed what it was made of when SCO claimed that Linux contained code that was illegally copied from SCO. While other IT publications at first accepted SCO's allegations as the truth, from day one the LWN editors knew what was what. When SCO published two examples of code sections 'illegally copied into Linux', Bruce Perens and the readers of LWN were able, in less than a day, to trace the real origins of the relevant source codes and prove that one of them was a product of the seventies and, ironically, the other was written by the Open Source community and illegally copied by SCO.

Investigative journalism had shown that it was worth the price.

Verdict: The Open Source community has been criticized for taking a free ride in the world of IT. There is much talk of freedom, but nobody is willing to pay for anything, opponents claim. If nothing else, the LWN case showed that this is simply not true. Linux users may not be prepared to hand over their cash to monopolies whose prices are 90 per cent air. No way are they ready to give up their basic freedoms, such as the free sharing of source code. But they are willing to pay for something that is of real importance to them. The $25,000 in LWN's account proved that.

We'd like to pay, please (Mandrake Club)

Because I did my compulsory military service in the non-combatant or civilian service, the story of the birth of Mandrake Linux has always fascinated me. The founder of MandrakeSoft, Gaël Duval, has said that the idea of a Linux distribution of his own was born in 1997 when he was doing his civilian service and consequently had a lot of spare time. That sounds familiar, but for some reason I never came up with an idea to fill my hours by founding a company that would change the world.

Of the four major Linux brands, *Mandrake* is clearly the youngest. Gaël released his first Mandrake Linux in the summer of 1998. He was a fan of the KDE desktop environment, which had just seen the release of the 1.0 version. The then market leader Red Hat hadn't made KDE part of its Linux, because there were some political differences about the licensing of Trolltech's Qt library, which KDE used.[56] Gaël took Red Hat's then 5.1 version, added KDE to it together with some other additions. He put the package he had onto a public Ftp server, called it *Linux-Mandrake 5.1*, and went off on a two-week summer holiday.

When he returned, his mailbox was full of enthusiastic responses! It was clear that 'Red Hat with KDE' had tapped into a need. With Frédéric Bastok and Jacques Le Marois, Gaël founded a company called MandrakeSoft to continue the work with Mandrake Linux, and by 1999 Mandrake was one of the most popular Linux versions, winning several awards and honorary mentions and finally, in 2000, achieving the same sales figures in the US as the market leader Red Hat.

The third quarter of 1999 generated a profit of €100,000. Not bad for a little company celebrating its first birthday! But that would be the last profit-making quarter in the Mandrake books for a long time to come.

Because this was 'new economy' madness at its most heated, Mandrake enjoyed the wheelbarrows of money that venture capitalists brought to the company's door. In interviews, Gaël spoke of listing the company on the Nasdaq. With new investors, the company also got a new management, whose job it was to make the money invested in the company work. A lot of new programmers were employed to further the development of the company's popular Linux distribution. Money was also invested in new fields, such as Linux training and eLearning in particular. Education on the Web was one of the big things among the businessmen of the 'new economy' in the year 2000.

The 'world-class management team' – as Gaël was later to describe the leadership in sarcastic tones – worked hard. Mandrake's turnover grew quickly, but unfortunately mostly on the expenditure side. Only a year after the first quarter being in the black, the company had a quarter that made a loss of €3 million, achieving an even worse quarter the next year: €5 million in the red!

---

56 Qt was not at the time being distributed under the GPL licence, which is why for several years the entire KDE project incurred the wrath of Richard Stallman's Free Software Foundation.

When the new management had the bright idea to 'cut losses' by dropping the development of the company's own Linux distribution, in order to focus on eLearning, the original owners reached breaking point. The management was told to pack their bags, and Gaël once again took control.

From the start, Red Hat had been very loyal to the Free Software ideology and published all its programs under the GPL licence, but Mandrake went even further. Red Hat used to release excerpts of its future Linuxes in a package called Rawhide. However, Mandrake opened up the entire development process to interested independent hackers. Through mailing lists set up for the purpose, anybody could get involved in planning the future of Mandrake Linux. In addition to good ideas, the company also accepts code from volunteers, although their own employees, of course, do most of the work.

Does this sound Utopian? Would you do something for free, hand it over to a company, then buy the product they make from it back from them? It doesn't sound very likely, but already in the first year more than 200 eager hackers were involved in the Cooker project. Whether that's such a good name for the project is another question, considering the old adage about too many cooks spoiling the broth. Nonetheless, it's thanks to this strategy that Mandrake Linux has always been very close to its users and striven to respond to their needs – and after all that's what Open Source is all about.

From the start, part of the Mandrake strategy was to make the latest Mandrake version available on the Internet as soon as it was ready.[57] This set it apart – in a good way – from Red Hat, which at the time used to delay the release of its online version until the physical CDs had reached the stores. In a number of interviews Gaël said he thought it was good for the company to make the new version available on the Web as soon as possible, rather than artificially (mean-spiritedly) withholding it for months. And that way of doing things was also in line with the principles of openness.

The Mandrake strategy must have played a part in its rapid growth in popularity. But one would expect such a strategy to have had a negative impact on the sale of the physical CDs, which were always late. However, the most loyal users understood the principle of reciprocity, and as soon as

---

57 The company made an exception to this principle in the autumn of 2003, when it released the 9.2 version. At first, Mandrake 9.2 was available only to members of the Mandrake Club and was only released for completely free distribution at the same time as the CDs became available.

the CDs were available they went and bought them just to support the future of their favourite Linux. Besides which they were happy to pay for such a good product. The CDs themselves were obviously of no use to them, since they'd already been using the downloadable version for several months. They just happened to understand that without any revenue their favourite Linux couldn't stay around for long.

This principle of reciprocity gradually grew into the idea for a new business model: the *Mandrake Club*. CDs are slow to manufacture, and many of the buyers didn't even need them; they only bought them to support Mandrake. So, why bother them with having to buy the CD at all, since the manufacture, packaging, and physical distribution of CDs all costs money. The Mandrake Club is for Mandrake users, who pay what is essentially an annual subscription fee ranging from $60 to $1,200, with most users paying either $60 or $120 a year.

There are some practical benefits to being in the club. Using your Mandrake Club password you can download versions of Java, RealPlayer, Flash, Acrobat and other programs that have been adapted for Mandrake; programs that are free but not freely distributable. Without the club, a Mandrake user would have to surf the Internet to pick up the same programs and install them one at a time. A feature that has proved very popular among club members is RPM Voting – the chance to vote on which Open Source programs should be included in the next version of Mandrake Linux. This allows even those Mandrake users who lack the level of programming skills necessary to participate in Cooker to influence the future of their Linux distribution. But, in addition to this and some other relatively small benefits, there is no actual reason to pay the membership fee.

Briefly, Gaël Duval's argument for the Mandrake Club was: 'Following the principles of the Free Software ideology we wish to give you Mandrake Linux completely free, without any catches. We also want to give our products the necessary security updates freely and for free, without any catches. In the long run we won't be able to do this, however, unless somebody pays our employees. Therefore we ask that you support the Mandrake Linux, which we have given you for free, by joining the Mandrake Club.'

Once again, that sounds Utopian. Who would pay to belong to a club if there were no benefits to be had? As in the case of *Linux Weekly News*, the Mandrake Club has shown that Linux users are willing to pay for services they have enjoyed for free if the service or product is worth it. In 2003 the Mandrake Club had some 14,000 active members as well as a couple of corporate members (who pay a higher subscription fee).

That is a small number compared to the several million people who use Mandrake Linux. Even so, if each of those 14,000 users has paid an average membership fee of $120, that's $1.68 million a year, which is quite a lot for a company the size of MandrakeSoft! And the good thing about it is that the income goes directly to paying the salaries of the company's programmers, rather than to paying for the manufacture of superfluous CDs.

Although the company rid itself of the management team that had almost bankrupted it, some of the commitments they'd already made were not so easy to shake off. The eLearning deals, for instance, required payments to be made for years to come and despite MandrakeSoft severely streamlining its operations, the old sins cast long shadows in the form of many accounting quarters in the red. But Gaël's long-term commitment to the principle of openness had created a group of loyal Mandrake users and they were the ones who kept the company going through the hard times.

During the worst period Mandrake even had to beg its clients for donations. Mandrake never listed on Nasdaq, but at the end of 2001 the company stock was on sale, on the slightly less well-known French exchange Euronext, to the most loyal supporters of the company, its own customers. In the long run they may prove to be better owners than the 'world-class' venture capitalists. When the capital raised through the stock issue was spent and there were still bills to pay and commitments to honour, the company's founders had again to plead with its Mandrake users, who hurried to buy club membership and other company products. Again, in December 2002, the company asked its customers for support, and even this third time the Mandrake users supported them.

First the Mandrake Club, then the fundraising, and through it all Mandrake's customers remained staunchly loyal. In the tough IT business, not many companies would dare hope for so much from their customers, but as the Mandrake experience so clearly demonstrated, one does reap what one sows. From the outset, the company had been open and fair with its customers, and in return the customers helped it to survive.

Despite the help, MandrakeSoft had to apply for debt restructuring in January 2003 to protect itself from the last eLearning liabilities, which were due to be paid within the month. A little over a year after that the debt restructuring was completed and, even better, after a break of some five years the company again started to show a profit. With Red Hat moving away from the home users to focus on expensive corporate server architectures, many previous Red Hat users have become Mandrake customers and after a long break the company seems once again to be a strong Linux contender. Since the restructuring programme, their accounts have been consistently in the black, and in 2004 the company branched out from being the favourite Linux for home users to doing some rather more lucrative corporate business by making big Linux deals with two French government departments.

Verdict: MandrakeSoft has been the most open of the commercial Linux distributions and is strongly committed to the Free Software ideology. The company was born of its time, and survived the years of the Internet bubble which created a lot of froth for Mandrake. Through its Mandrake Club strategy the company built, on purpose, a business model similar to the one *Linux Weekly News* was later to chance upon. Both LWN and Mandrake are proof that if work is done openly, fairly, decently, and most of all if it's *of use*, then loyal customers will willingly pay and support it, even when it's in trouble.

Barn-raising and the clothesline paradox (Debian)

Part Three of this book has been looking at how Open Source companies survive financially. Among them we've looked at three of the four best-known brands of Linux: Red Hat, SuSE and Mandrake, but the job isn't done without looking at the fourth one: Debian.

Debian is not a company. Then how can it be considered as if it were a business model? Perhaps it can't. But Debian exists, and that can't be ignored. Not only does it exist, it's one of the oldest and most popular Linux versions and in many statistics it beats the competing Linux distributions hands down.

Have you ever installed a Windows machine or watched anyone else installing Windows? When the installation is complete, you have a computer that works, but no more than that.[58] Next, you have to install a word-

---

58 Well, of course some people think a computer with Windows installed on it instead of Linux is a computer with serious problems. But let's pretend you have a working computer.

processing program (OpenOffice, maybe) and an e-mail program (Mozilla, perhaps). But that is just the beginning. What if you need image processing software? And how about your printer – does it work? And are you planning to play games? They all have to be separately installed and you even have to get them from various vendors, since you're using closed software.

However, if you're using Linux and Free Software, all the software can all be conveniently bundled up in the same package. When you've installed Linux, you've also installed hundreds of other useful programs, including OpenOffice and Mozilla. Because the software can be freely distributed, your Linux distributor – whether it be Red Hat, SuSE, Mandrake, Debian or anyone else – has been able to gather everything you need into one package. And your Linux computer will be ready to use in less than an hour.

For anyone who measures their Linux by the number of programs that come with it, Debian includes 8,710 different software programs, which is by far the biggest.[59] And all this can be installed for free by downloading it from the Internet or alternatively from CDs that cost around €8 from DataClub. Imagine, 8,710 different programs, all nicely bundled up in an easily installable and working package.

The other Linux versions are usually only available for computers that have Intel's so-called x86 architecture and in some instances some other architectures, such as the PowerPC (Apple computers) or IA-64 (Intel's new 64 bit architecture) or AMD's Opteron. At least Red Hat and SuSE support IBM's mainframe architectures in addition to these. But Debian is in a league of its own. It works on eleven different architectures![60]

The Debian project currently involves almost 1,000 active programmers or hackers. The biggest Linux company, Red Hat, has some 600 employees and only some 300 of them are engineers.[61]

Debian is a non-commercial organization which involves the Debian-making programmers but also the people who run Debian's Web and data servers. In addition to which, there is of course someone who donated the servers themselves as well as their Internet connections, or at least the money needed for them. Then there's legal counsel – they, too, are

---

59   This statistic is from December 2003. The number has been growing rapidly in the past few years, so by the time you're reading this, there's bound to be a lot more.

60   By the time of going to press, this number too had grown.

61   You could argue, of course, that today IBM and HP are also Linux companies and they do have rather more employees.

volunteers – and the people who write manuals and make translations. And of course a large project like this always requires some bureaucracy – even in the world of Open Source – so Debian also has elected leaders.

Debian was founded in 1993 by *Ian Murdock*.[62] At the time, Linus Torvalds and company had got the kernel into such good shape that Linux could be used with other free programs on top of it. However, these separate free programming projects were spread any which way across the Internet and nobody had pulled them all together to make a unified operating source product. But in 1993 the first Linux distributions were born, and Debian was one of them.

Because the Linux kernel, the bash command interpreter, the GCC compiler, the Emacs editor and all the other tools required to make a perfect operating system, most of which had been created under the GNU project, had been developed through the open model, it was only natural for Ian Murdock to make his Linux distribution open too. The commercial Linux companies came into the picture a little later. And just as well – diversity and freedom are our guiding principles, remember?

And so, little by little, the Debian project started to develop, with an ever increasing number of volunteer hackers maintaining a growing collection of Free Software and a free OS. One of the early leaders of the project was Bruce Perens, who today is one of the best-known advocates of Open Source. One of Bruce's legacies is that Debian always offers a comprehensive range of software for radio amateurs.

The first 'ready' version of Debian was (exceptionally) given the version number 1.1, and that historic event took place in June 1996. At the time, many commercial companies, among them Red Hat and SuSE as well as the infamous Caldera, had a good head start in their released Linux versions.

Debian has by its mere existence balanced the Linux world, by offering a free alternative to the commercial Linux brands. Where most Linux companies release new versions of their Linuxes as often as twice a year, Debian can let up to two years pass without releasing a new version. Perhaps more than any of the other Linuxes, Debian has kept to the principle of releasing a product only 'when it's ready'. By the time Debian finally releases a new version, many of the programs included in it are already relatively old, because Debian observes a very conservative testing and quality control policy. In part, the delay also reflects the Debian principle of

---

62   If I tell you Ian's wife is called Debra, you can guess where the project got its name.

releasing for all eleven different architectures at the same time. Most other Linux distributions release the version for each of the architectures as they get them done.

Although many of us computer freaks love to try everything new on our computers, Debian's steady pace actually suits many people very well. In the corporate world – where people actually want to get some work done in between – it's a positive thing not to have to run around updating all the company computers so often. Besides which, Debian computer freaks aren't bothered by the slow pace, because many of them use the so-called 'testing' version of Debian. The 'testing' version is a continually evolving collection of software which finally becomes the next version of Debian. Although it's not an official version, it is of course publicly available – after all, this is an Open Source project![63]

Since it has at times been difficult to guess at what Red Hat and SuSE are planning, and with Mandrake's future being at stake due to financial problems, and many smaller Linux brands have genuinely disappeared, Debian's non-commercial status has actually seemed to give it a competitive edge. Debian hasn't suffered from financial problems, its plans haven't changed every six months and nobody has suddenly offered to buy Debian – not that it would be possible, anyway.

In addition to users who value stability, Debian is naturally of particular interest to programmers and computer freaks. This, among other things, is reflected in the installation of Debian. Whereas other Linux companies make their installation programs as automatic as possible and give them nice colours, Debian's installation program tends to ask fascinating questions, such as: 'What kernel driver file is needed by your network adapter?' or 'What is the refresh rate of your monitor?' Real nerds know no better fun than answering such questions, but ordinary mortals need a Linux that is as highly automated and colourful as possible.

As a giant project maintained by volunteers, Debian also realizes the Open Source principle of doing it together. For programmers and other real nerds – from Linus Torvalds down – it's always been more fun to make your own operating system rather than buy it encased in a colourful cardboard box.

---

63 The use of Debian's 'testing' and 'unstable' versions works in the same way as Mandrake's Cooker project. Actually, Debian was the model for Mandrake in this respect.

In this sense, Debian resembles the Finnish *talkoo* or barn-raising tradition. A Finnish *talkoot* [sic] is arranged when a Finn wishes to build, say, a summer cottage by a nice lake. What he does *not* do is to buy a ready-made cabin to be delivered to the site on a trailer. Where's the fun in that? No, the cottage is built using *talkoo* power. A *talkoot* is when someone gets all their mates and a few barely-known acquaintances together to build the cottage as a joint effort. The future hostess of the cottage serves the *talkoo* workers soup, and it's all a bit like barn-raising in the Amish culture. Except that the Finns obviously head to the sauna when the building work is done, and are also likely to down a beer or two at the end of the day.

The Debian project is like an enormous virtual barn-raising. Volunteers often gather on Internet Relay Chat (IRC) channels and work together to write the code for the new programs in Debian. While they're coding away they also chat about this and that, some of it related to Debian, some not. They're doing it together and having fun. Somebody may even have a beer and give the glass a virtual clink to drink to the success of it all. And alongside the fun, they create the best operating system in the world.[64]

But let's go back for a moment to Debian as a business model. Can we call *barn-raising* a business model? The unspoken assumption in this part of the book has been that one must be able to build a profitable business on Linux for the idea of Open Source to be viable. Debian (and Eclipse, Blender, Mozilla, and many other examples in this part of the book) prove that assumption wrong. Debian exists and is widely used, but it is not a business that is out to, well, do business.

Those of us who've spent years in an over-commercialized capitalist (mean-spirited) world seem to have forgotten that not everything can be measured in monetary terms. (And I'm not talking here about friendship, love, and the like, but actual material things.) There's a tendency to think that because Microsoft has such a huge turnover, then it must logically follow that Windows is a good operating system. But what is Debian's turnover? It doesn't even have one.

To equate profit with quality is to forget that the actual job of computer programs is *not* to increase turnover, but rather to produce books, letters, minutes of meetings, images, films, web pages, music, phone books, statements of accounts, payslips, information storage, to enable

---

64   You can get to know the people working on Debian through the IRC channels on at:
      http://www.linuks.mine.nu/debian-faq/

communication, space travel, and much else besides. And Debian, for instance, makes all that possible, including having been used on a space shuttle! So, Debian is a useful and meaningful thing – but not a business model.

Because many of us get locked into a certain way of thinking we can miss obvious connections and solutions. Twenty years ago, solar architect Steve Baer came up with a good metaphor for our inability to perceive locally available solutions. He called it the *clothesline paradox*. It goes like this: if I were to buy an electric clothes-drier, that purchase would show up on a statistic somewhere, from which someone would eventually infer that electricity consumption had increased in Finland. And so I will have made it that bit harder for Finland to keep within the limits set by the Kyoto Protocol to tackle climate change.[65]

If, however, I get rid of my clothes-drier and let my clothes dry on a clothesline, there's no statistic that says Finland is now using more solar energy. But that doesn't mean a clothesline isn't a good way to dry clothes. And there we have the *clothesline paradox*.

The old Debian activist Bruce Perens understood the lesson of the clothesline paradox. From the point of view of Linux users, it's not relevant how many operating systems they have bought. What matters is that the work which needs doing, can get done. Some business leaders who met Bruce have apparently realized the same thing, because at the request of some, as yet unnamed, clients, Bruce has recently begun working on a new Linux distribution called UserLinux. Its aim is not to sell as many copies of Linux as possible, nor is it the aim of UserLinux users to buy as many Linuxes as possible. What they do want, however, is to get their job done. The aim of UserLinux is to be a Linux distribution which, like Debian, is open to everybody, but also to be a more streamlined Linux version than Debian, to be more automated – for corporate clients.

At the time of writing, UserLinux was still just a 'twinkle in Bruce's eye' and it remains to be seen how the project is realized. Red Hat's latest changes in its range and pricing are sure to have been instrumental in getting the debate about UserLinux going, and getting the organizations behind the project to see the benefits of a model such as Debian. *'I know of one business that invested millions into developing the IA-64 Linux system, with*

---

65 American readers of this English edition can rest assured they have nothing to worry about in this regard. Their Texas-born president never signed the Kyoto Protocol, so you can all keep on using electricity regardless of climate change.

a marked absence of help from Red Hat. Now, that business is forced to buy their own software back from Red Hat at a high per-unit price, to package with their own products.' [66] The project gets some credibility from the fact that the organizations backing it, according to Bruce, have pledged to finance UserLinux to the tune of one million dollars a year, and that these organizations have a total of some 50,000 computers. So, this is no longer just hackers getting together for some barn-raising and fun, this is big corporations wanting to get the job done.

Verdict: Debian is doubly Open Source. All the programs it contains are created using the Open Source development model. In addition to which Debian itself was born as Open Source. A thousand volunteers worked to develop Debian, which in many ways is the biggest Linux distribution. In the IT market of the early 2000s, Debian has even been the most financially stable alternative for Linux users. From the criteria applied throughout this book, there is simply nothing bad to say about Debian.

Glass House, a totally transparent company (fictitious)

In the case of Mandrake and *Linux Weekly News*, when clients are prepared to support a company financially in exchange for 'nothing', i.e. not in return for certain products, one of the key issues has become how to report back to those clients on the company's financial situation. The message from the clients is clear: 'We're happy to support you, but you must tell us how much money you need.' Some have even suggested that the companies make their entire accounts public, so that everyone has free access to check up on anything and to gain a clear picture of the company's financial situation at any given time.

I've yet to hear of any company that has actually done this, and for a listed company it may not be easy to do, as there are strict rules about what information they can and must give, and when. However, the thought itself is intriguing. It may not be completely realistic, and it is not directly connected to Open Source, but let's use the rest of Part Three on this mind

---

66   Although Bruce Perens does not reveal the identity of the company which invested
millions, it was Hewlett-Packard.
And, remember that selling one licence per computer is rare in the world of Open
Source.

game. If a company wanted to be as open as possible, how open could it be and what would it lead to?

Although the question is carried to the extreme, it is not entirely without precedent. Nokia, for instance, was cited earlier in this book as an example of a company that is sadly enamoured with non-disclosure agreements. However, the passion for keeping secrets is not something the company carries into every area. In its relationship with its subcontractors Nokia strives to make the information flow both ways as smoothly and openly as possible.[67] If, for instance, a subcontractor could follow the sales figures for mobile phones by directly tapping into Nokia's databases, the subcontractor could prepare for the increased demand in advance, before the actual order comes in from Nokia. This would remove a number of bottlenecks and make the long and complex chain of production run more smoothly.

So, there is a realistic argument to be made for open thinking. But how open could a company be and what would it lead to? Now that IT companies are building their head offices from Plexiglas, it's about time we tried a thought experiment: What would a totally transparent company be like?

Our totally transparent company wouldn't necessarily be in the IT field, but the product would naturally follow the spirit of Open Source whenever appropriate.[68] That goes without saying. But what else?

Well, first of all, it would obviously not have a single trade secret. Non-disclosure agreements would be banned. Like Mandrake's Cooker, product development would be open, with company e-mailing lists open to people outside the company.

Budgets and financial accounts would be open to public scrutiny insofar as it's possible and makes sense. Naturally, for reasons of confidentiality, the salaries and sick days of individual workers could not be made public, but otherwise everything would be out in the open.

In addition to product development, the company's board meetings and other negotiations at management level would also be publicly accessible. And I don't mean just the final decisions, but also any vetoed ideas and

---

67   Well, if we're honest, we must admit that the culture of secrecy and mean-spiritedness is so strong in all of us that it's not always so easy to create such a culture of open information, but at least in theory Nokia is as open as possible towards its subcontractors.

68   The next section of the book will deal with the use of the Open Source ideology outside the IT sector.

other suggestions that have been put forward would all be recorded and made accessible – the meetings could, for instance, be video-taped.

If a company were to meet such demands for 100 per cent openness, it would become a totally transparent company. What a contrast to all the 'Enrons' of today to whose tune the financial world dances. Office buildings of Plexiglas may look transparent, but actually even the glass walls are less than see-through, as from the outside they reflect the external light rather than what goes on inside. Our fictional company, on the other hand, would be a true, genuinely transparent *Glass House*.

So, what would happen to this transparent company? If the observations we've made of the Open Source world are reliable, the open processes in the product development of the company and its management would surely open up the company for some surprises in the form of help from the outside. That would accelerate product development and over time make it better than its competition. The company could form totally new kinds of partnerships, or perhaps its clients would come up with suggestions for reorganizing its sales methods, just as outsiders send in suggestions for improvements to the code for Open Source programming projects.

Of course, the Open Source product would also be available to the competition, which would be a challenge for our transparent company. A company which works to the principles of openness cannot hide behind copyright, patents, trade secrets and other traditional models of mean-spiritedness, but must be prepared to face competition openly. That would not only keep the company on its toes at all times but also force it to continually evolve and renew itself. Of course, such declarations are endlessly repeated like some kind of mantra by most companies, but in an *open* business such aims would become real requirements.

Total transparency would also lead to some surprising and possibly difficult situations, which would require the company to look at the basics of business from a new perspective – a bit like when Open Source was a new concept and the first Linux companies had to reassess their ways of working in the IT field.

An example of the kind of situation that would require new thinking might be when a client invites tenders from several potential business associates and specifies a certain day for receiving bids. First, the tenders are kept secret and not opened until the deadline is reached, at which point the client usually chooses the cheapest alternative. Because of the secrecy surrounding the tendering process, nobody can know for certain what their competitors will bid. Naturally, the point of all this is for the client inviting the tenders to get a product or service supplied as cheaply as possible.

Working to the principles of openness in such a competitive situation, our transparent company would inevitably be worse off than the others. While the closed companies would submit secret tenders, our transparent company would be open to having the minutes of its management meetings examined by their competitors, who would not only discover exactly what sum our company had tendered but perhaps even what detailed calculations had led up to it. Naturally, in such a situation, it would be ridiculously easy for a competitor to put in a lower tender.

This may mean that our open business would lose a lot of tenders. But, it's not quite that simple. The problem with inviting tenders is that there is a sort of gamble built into the law of supply and demand, because no party selling a product or service ever makes tenders purely on the basis of actual costs. Instead, they try to second-guess what the competing parties will tender, then formulate their own on the basis of that. They aim to strike a balance between making the tender as high as possible, yet lower than those of the competition, so that their produce or service is the one that wins the job and them the highest possible profit margin. Which is why many offers aren't necessarily as low as they could be.

Our open and transparent company could therefore protect itself by always and only submitting *honest* tenders! Honesty here means that our company would base its tenders only on the actual cost of the work involved, then honestly put in a tender that is as low as possible without actually losing money on the deal. If somebody makes an even lower offer, there's no reason to cry over the lost deal, because selling our product or service for less than our tendered amount would not have been good for us anyway. And it might just be that our tender is as low as anyone can go. If so, we've won honestly, without hiding anything at all!

If one looks at the situation from the point of view of the client requiring the service or product, for them to work with a company that always plays an open card would be to work with an ideal partner. Naturally it's not good for the client when tenders are based mostly on the competing companies guessing at how fat a deal they all think they can fool the client company into paying this time. A company that has calculated its tender openly is much easier to trust. If I were to receive an honest tender of €1,000,000 from a company that operated with open principles, and the tender from a closed company came in at €999,500, I'm likely to laugh at the latter and accept the former.

Verdict: The Glass House was an entirely fictitious company invented to exemplify what can follow from openness. Who am I to judge whether or not my ideas are good or bad? The aim of this book is to stimulate different ways of thinking about business, but also to encourage readers to increasingly apply open thinking in their own lives.

Summary

Part Three of this book has presented a number of case studies of companies and organizations in the Open Source world. Challenging traditional IT businesses through the rules of openness has forced the players in this sector to reassess their ways of doing business, which in turn has given rise to new and successful innovations in business. In the case of *Linux Weekly News*, for instance, it wasn't so much a question of the Open Source ideology, but the natural openness of the Internet and how to react with that. On the other hand, Debian and the clothesline paradox can help us understand that it may be hard to find the right answer because we've yet to ask all the right questions.

I've tried to judge each example according to how successful a company has been financially, together with how well the example follows the principles of the Open Source ideology. I thought it would be useful to sum up the results of this long section in a picture, which as we all know will say more than a thousand words.[69] You'll find the financially successful examples from this section of the book towards the top of graphic, and the less successful ones towards the bottom. The examples that follow the principles of Open Source are on the right, and the mean-spirited ones are to the left.

---

[69] Of course, this part of the book already has over 30,000 words – my computer can calculate that all on its own, isn't that marvellous – but I hope the graphic is of some use anyway.

Mean-spirited, but not too greedy (Sun and Java) Sell a selection of Open Source software on CD, but then restrict copying terms (SuSE) Mean-spirited, but not too greedy (Ghostscript) Selling closed source software in an Open Source environment (Ximian, Codeweavers, Transgaming)	Dual licensing (MySQL, Trolltech) Barn-raising and the clothesline paradox (Debian) Be the best expert in your field (SuSE) Pay for work (Germany & Kroupware) The patron and the artist (Larry Wall, Linus Torvalds, KDE) You need a piece of software, but it can't be developed as a closed source product (Mozilla, Eclipse, Blender...) Pay for work (Kolab, JBoss) Sell selected Open Source software on CD (Red Hat, and many others) Publish source code for an old game that's no longer sold (Quake) Give your product away but have subscribers so you can continue doing so (Mandrake, LWN)
Try really hard, alone, instead of cooperating (Corel)	Pay for work (Stephen King, the tip model, job market)

Part Four

in which *Harry Potter* is magically translated into German, ants screw up, Google gets competition, and the tangible meets the intangible.

Open Life

Rob McEwen wasn't the son of a gold miner, but his father often told him stories of the gold fever in the nineteenth century. Perhaps these stories played a part in Rob's 1989 decision to leave his job as an investment advisor and become a majority owner in a gold mine in the Red Lake region of Ontario.

Unfortunately, although Rob's gold mine was suffering, it wasn't from gold fever. Mining costs were high and the price of gold on the world market was low. To make matters worse, the miners went on strike. However, Rob didn't lose faith in his mine. Some 18 million ounces of gold had been mined in the Red Lake area and a mine close to Rob's had produced 10 million ounces. So far, only 3 million ounces had come out of Rob's mine, but he remained convinced that the same lode, or vein, must continue into his mine. They only needed to discover where!

In 1999, Rob attended an IT seminar at Massachusetts Institute of Technology (MIT). As it happened, one of the topics was Linux and a new and revolutionary way of making software. Rob got excited. This Open Source thing was just what his gold mine needed!

So in March 2000, Rob went public with a competition called the Goldcorp Challenge. All the data generated over the years of working the mine was published on the competition website, and the task for the entrants was to predict where the company should next drill their mine. The competition was open to everyone and in total the prizes amounted to $575,000.

Rob's idea was unheard of in the mining world. Every gold miner knows never to talk to anyone about their findings – they'd rather take their mining secrets to the grave. To begin with, Rob's own geologists were against his plan. Revealing the mine's data might, for instance, lure buyers into trying to wrest the mine away from Rob and the other owners. For a number of reasons, showing your cards in the mining business wasn't a good idea. Or so people had learned to believe.

Even so, the Goldcorp Challenge proved a success. Naturally, researchers from around the world were interested in this unique opportunity to gain access to the data from a genuine mine. Interested scientists from more than 50 countries visited the site, and files were downloaded more than 1,400 times. Eventually, the competition judges chose a virtual three-dimensional model of the mine created by two Australian companies – Fractal Graphics and Taylor Wall & Associates – as the winner. Using their model the Australians, who had never set foot in Canada, could predict where gold would next be found. Their prize was $105,000.

So what happened to Rob's mine? Did he hit the mother lode of Open Source? So far, Rob's company has mined where indicated by four of the five winning entries, and each one has proved its worth. In 1996, the Red Lake mine produced some 53,000 ounces with a production cost of $360 per ounce. In 2001 – the first post-competition year – they mined 500,000 ounces of gold and as the ore was richer than those they'd previously mined, the production price per ounce of gold was just $59. As the price of gold on the world market was $307 per ounce, the company made a big profit. In contrast, continuing with the old methods and production costs would not have been possible at such a low selling price. Without Rob's Open Source idea and the Goldcorp Challenge, the mine may well have been shut down.[70]

In this final part of the book I will extend the idea of openness in the world of computers into the world we live in. As Rob's experience demonstrated, openness can be made to work even in the mining of gold. Where else might openness be beneficial? Like the tale of Rob and his golden challenge, many of the stories in this section are from real life. Others are suggestions, parts of the open revolution that have yet to be realized. However, it is important to remember that they are all just examples: the point of Rob's and the other stories is to show that the Open Source way of thinking can be applied anywhere.

Rob's story has nothing to do with Linux or computers, but it does tell us that Open Source need not only be the special privilege of computer programmers. By challenging, through open thinking, the conventions of mean-spirited secrecy we can all be as revolutionary in our own fields as Richard Stallman and Linus Torvalds have been as programmers and Rob McEwen as a gold miner. Through open thinking, you can hit gold – literally! We already have open code, but why settle for that when there's so much more on offer? It's only a matter of altering our ways of thinking, of doing various everyday things and of living our everyday life. And that life can be an Open Life.

---

70 Rob's story was told by the Web edition of the *Fast Company* magazine in June 2002: http://www.fastcompany.com/online/59/mcewen.html

Literature

The 'ownership' of software is based on copyright law, and the General Public Licence (GPL) formulated by Richard Stallman is based on a new application of this law. In consequence, one might think this Open Source thinking could be applied to other works that fall under copyright law. And of course that has already been done. First, there was literature.

The invention of the printing press is what prompted the evolution that led to the copyright laws we have today, which makes it a natural starting point. Financing book publishing also resembles the software industry in a number of other ways. The actual creative work is in writing the book, after which any number of copies can be printed – not for free, perhaps, but at a reasonable unit cost. In today's Internet world, it's naturally also possible to distribute a book in digital form, which truly does make copying costs nonexistent.

So, why aren't books published according to the principles of Open Source? Perhaps the reason is simple: people don't think of doing it.

On the other hand, it might also be that Open Source doesn't give quite the same edge in writing a book as it does in computer programming. After all, writing software is usually a very complex process which requires the input, often of hundreds, of people for several years. In this complex process the benefits of openness compared to closed systems is obvious (as is proved by Linux, Apache, etc.).

Writing a book, then, is not so complicated. Actually, your average book can be written by one author, and it doesn't necessarily have to take even a whole year (provided you don't write only at the weekends, in addition to having a day job, which is how I wrote this book). But to collaborate with others to write a book, one would have to be able to divide the workload in some sensible way, and for many books this would be very difficult. If it were fiction, for instance, the writers would have to discuss their plot very carefully, agree on characters and so on, in order for the story to be told with any coherence. In the end, it would be far easier for one person to write the book on their own.

Even so, Open Source books do exist. But rather than being plot-thick detective stories they are more likely to be, for instance, Linux manuals.[71]

At a very early stage, when the first GNU books were beginning to take off, it was clear that a free program should naturally have a free manual. And behold, writing manuals works fine within the framework of the Open Source process. It's easy enough to divide the parts of a manual for a number of writers to work on. Another benefit is that there's usually a need to update the manual whenever a program changes and evolves. This too makes an Open Source manual better than something not just anybody can change, as most of the old manual can usually be employed in the revised one. It's only necessary to change the parts that relate to what has changed in the new version of the software, to add new chapters for the new features, without having to rewrite the whole book. Such a process would be more complicated with conventional books under current copyright law, which would not allow an out-of-date manual to be updated without permission of its original author/s. Which is why members of the Open Source community always include a text specifically granting this permission to all and sundry every time they release a manual or the code for a program.

And because that is likely to discomfit a lot of publishers, this is a good place to reiterate what has been said about software in earlier chapters. There are bound to be people who feel that publishing a book on the Internet under Open Source terms is a bad idea and will be the ruin of the publishing industry. But this is roughly the same thought that struck traditional software businesses when they first heard of Linux. In actual fact, the situation is the reverse. An Open Source book which is available on the Internet is like free money for a publisher. It's a book that is already written and only needs to be printed for the money to start rolling in. And lots of smart publishers have actually realized that. Apparently, the publisher of most Open Source books is O'Reilly, the same publishing house that once upon a time put Larry Wall, the creator of the programming language Perl, on its payroll and thereby gained its role as purveyor of books to the Open

---

71 Linus Torvalds' grandfather, Ole Torvalds, was actually involved in a detective story collaboration with a number of other Finnish authors writing in Swedish. Each author wrote one chapter, but there was no discussion of plot or characters; the manuscript was simply handed on to the next writer, who had to come up with a way of moving the so-called plot forward. The collaborative book was published in 1950, but it was *not* a bestseller. The title *Den rödgröna skorpionen*, which translates as *The Red-Green Scorpion*, may have had something to do with that, as it's a title that sounds almost as classy in Swedish as it does in English!

Source movement. But O'Reilly is not the only publisher to discover the Open Source market. Prentice Hall actively seeks Open Source writers for a series which has as its Series Editor the spokesperson of the Open Source community, Bruce Perens.

So there are some Open Source books. But we've slid back into the field of Linux. So is there any other Open Source literature outside Linux manuals?

Harry Potter and the magic of Open Source

In the autumn of 2003, a news item about German *Harry Potter* fans caught my eye. In June of that year, *Harry Potter and the Order of the Phoenix*, fifth in the series of books so beloved by children, youth and adults, had been published.

At least, that's when the English-language edition was published. The German edition, having yet to be translated, would have come out some time after it. But a true fan, rather than wait for the German edition, would rush out and buy the English edition, then spell their way through the latest adventure in the original language. On publication of the German edition, it too would be acquired by the fan.

That might be enough for your ordinary run-of-the-mill kind of a fan, but *true* true fans take their commitment even further. They do the translation themselves. And, naturally, they cooperate with other fans to get it done quickly.

Not long after the publication of *Order of the Phoenix* in English, more than a thousand German *Harry Potter* fans were organized on the website www.harry-auf-deutsch.de. The average age of these volunteer translators was sixteen, and many of them had done only two or three years of English at school.

The job was divided into five-page sections. Some volunteers took part by proofreading the texts translated by others, and also by commenting on alternative translations. To translate the vocabulary specific to the magical world created by J.K. Rowling, a *Harry Potter* English/German dictionary was set up on the site. A lively debate then ensued about the translations offered in the dictionary. For instance, how does one translate the word *squib* (a person whose parents are wizards, yet he or she is born with no magical powers)?

As you might expect, the project quickly ran into the German publisher's lawyers, because the law prohibits the circulation of unofficial translations of a book over the Internet without the permission of the originating author, usually via their publisher or agent. Fortunately, the Harry-auf-Deutsch website was able to make peace with the German publisher by making the site a closed club. Thus, the final result of the translation effort isn't available to all and sundry, but only for sharing among those who partook in the work.

Harry Potter fans in other countries didn't fare so well. For instance, fans in the Czech Republic also tired of the nine-month wait for the official translation. So, like their fellow fans in Germany, they too produced an unofficial version much sooner. But the site hosting the Czech translation was closed down by the publisher in possession of the Czech rights to *Harry Potter*. Naturally, this incurred the wrath of the same young book buyers whom the publisher wanted to woo.

Although such *Potter* translations stretch the limits of copyright law, they do also show the power of Open Source thinking. Where most professional translators spend almost a year translating one novel a group of hundreds or even thousands of volunteer translators could get the job done in a couple of months – or weeks, if less proficient work was acceptable. And the overall quality of the translation needn't really suffer compared to a professional translation. Quite the opposite. If the magic of the Linux phenomenon can be applied to the translation of a novel, it just might be rather exciting to read an Open Source version well *before* the closed and official published version had come out.

With *Harry Potter*, J.K. Rowling may have inadvertently inspired a way of translating books that suits the Internet age, but the young wizard has also taken over the number one spot in a more traditional literary sub-culture. For a long time, so called *fan fiction* literature has offered popular characters in novels and films a life outside their published stories. In a fan-fiction story a well-known character from a series of books or a TV series takes part in fresh adventures written by someone other than the character's creator. Such stories are written as a hobby by loyal fans of the character. Often enough, fan fiction is written in a short story format, but it is fairly common for such fans to write whole unofficial novels. But again, I must stress the words 'as a hobby', because selling a story based on someone else's character without the permission of the original creator would be plagiarism and therefore an infringement of their copyright. Actually, it's not exactly legal to distribute the stories over the Internet either even if they are made available free for others to read, but that doesn't seem to bother these fans.

Naturally, the Internet has given the whole fan fiction culture a boost. A popular site for fans of fan fiction, called www.fanfiction.net, publishes new stories on a daily basis. Last time I checked, Alexandre Dumas' three musketeers were fencing their way through an additional 42 stories, Sherlock Holmes solves 347 previously unpublished mysteries, and there are even 91 fan-fiction stories about Homer Simpson. With 8,800 stories, for a long time *Star Wars* was the undisputed leader but now, nobody can touch *Harry Potter* – with over a hundred thousand fan-fiction stories, wands have left light sabres far behind. You can read what Harry does during his summer vacations between his term-time activities at Hogwarts in the official stories by J.K. Rowling, or what happens when Harry grows up and goes to university![72]

Wikipedia, an extremely open encyclopedia

Although most books are best written by one person, there are other kinds of publications that typically have more than one author – sometimes very many. Encyclopedias are one such important category.

Unlike *Harry Potter* and other novels, encyclopedias are a compilation of independent articles. Many different experts are asked to write articles related to their particular area of expertise. And because the articles for an encyclopedia don't need to be written in any particular order, all participants can be working on it at the same time. So it would seem that an encyclopedia could be compiled and published using Open Source methods. You may not be surprised to learn that there is such an encyclopedia.

Thirty-seven-year-old Jimmy Wales, a fan of Linus Torvalds and Richard Stallman, had a vision of his own for an Open Source project. Since Jimmy knew something about the dynamics of an Open Source project, he

---

72   ...where, among other things, Harry begins dating. The R-rated stories are a popular form of fan fiction.

also realized that compiling an encyclopedia would fit the ideology of Open Source very well. So, in 1999 he founded the *Nupedia* project.

However, *Nupedia* didn't become what Jimmy had planned. Over a period of two years, the project swallowed a significant amount in grants and resulted in the publication of just twelve articles. Twelve articles in two years! So what went wrong?

In theory, the *Nupedia* project was open to all – *anybody* could contribute articles for it. In reality, you couldn't just sign up and become a contributor. If you wanted to write an article about something you had to send in an application, which had to be approved at some point, somewhere. All articles were checked and rewritten several times, by other experts – because that is how encyclopedias are usually written. And after two years, only twelve articles had passed this scrutiny! Obviously, that is not how to organize an Open Source project.[73]

In January 2001, the failed *Nupedia* was replaced by *Wikipedia*.[74] It used the WikiWikiWeb technology which became widespread in the late nineties. A wiki is a web page that users themselves can read, write, and edit. Originally, wikis were used for group work or on Intranet pages used within a company, but *Wikipedia* has certainly proved what good use this technology can be put to on the Internet, where everybody has access to the pages.

In a wiki, each page has, for instance, a link at the end that allows users to edit the page immediately. And they don't even need to have a special program to do it – the page they want to edit opens up in the user's own web browser.[75] In some cases, no user ID is needed to enable anyone to edit the page, but even where an ID is required it is only necessary to register, and as soon as that is done you are free to edit the page. Trouble-free participation in the editing process is crucial, as all sorts of checking, pre-censoring, and approval of new users is anathema.

---

73   So, how should an Open Source project be organized to make it as successful as possible? See Eric S. Raymond's famous essay 'The Cathedral and the Bazaar': http://www.catb.org/~esr/writings/cathedral-bazaar/

74   http://wikipedia.org/

75   Typically, html code is not used when creating a wiki page, as that would be too difficult for an average web surfer. Instead, the contents of the page are written in a very simple code that resembles ordinary text and which the wiki program then converts into an html page.

Most people react with incredulity when they first hear of wiki technology. Surely it can't work for real! I admit I thought that myself, a long time ago.

If a page can be changed freely by anyone on the public Internet, isn't that asking for trouble? You might expect all sorts of vandals would be rushing in their hordes to make the most of this opportunity.

But despite access and efficiency being central to the wiki philosophy, when it comes to giving people their chance to contribute, this doesn't necessarily mean that no checking is ever done. In addition to writing new articles, the vast army of volunteers involved in the creation of *Wikipedia* are also involved in checking the changes that are made. On an encyclopedia site it is necessary to make sure the facts are right and that everything gets proofread, which is just as important as writing the articles themselves.

All wiki programs have convenient tools to make checking easier. All the latest changes are found centrally on a page of their own, which makes it easy to look them over. The Diff tool shows all changes, which means you don't have to read the entire page again if you don't want to. And if the changes were done out of malice or you just don't happen to like them, then changing things back is just as easy and accessible to everybody as it was to make the changes in the first place.

Of course there is some vandalism, but attempts to ruin things for others tend to be very short-lived. The vandals are so outnumbered by those who take the creation of the encyclopedia seriously that you rarely see the troubles in *Wikipedia* before they're gone. But some targets are just too tempting for mischief-makers. Today, you are no longer free to change the front page of the *Wikipedia* site, because it became a sport for some people to insert large pictures of penises on it.

Ants are a classic example of diligent workers. This is something that parents want to show their children, at some point taking them to an ant hill to gaze in wonder at how big a hill the tiny ants have built. (The lesson being that teamwork makes greater things possible, and that one should work hard... But you'll know all this because you too were taken to watch ants.)

I once read somewhere about a study which showed that about 20 per cent of the ants in an anthill do totally stupid things, such as tear down walls the other ants have just built, or take recently gathered food and stow it where none of them will ever find it, or do other things to sabotage

149

everything the other ants so diligently try to achieve. The theory is that these ants don't do these things out of malice but simply because they're stupid.[76]

I expect you're thinking what I'm thinking, which is that you know of some human organizations in which the behaviour of at least 20 per cent of the people in them is just as idiotic! And that's why many of our organizations formulate ways of preventing the kind of problems that plague ant colonies. If a number of people do some stupid thing, we make a rule to say it mustn't be done. Then we need a rule that says everybody has to read the rules. Before long, we need managers and inspectors to make sure people read and follow the rules and that nobody does anything stupid, even by mistake. Finally, the organization has a large group of people who spend their time thinking up and writing rules, and enforcing them. And those not involved in doing that are primarily concerned with not breaking the rules, which means they do what they should be doing very carefully.

Critics of Open Source projects claim that their non-existent hierarchy and lack of organization leads to inefficiency. With nobody overseeing the whole, a number of people may inadvertently do the same work and others might do something totally unnecessary, something nobody will ever need. Instinct tells us that to avoid such problems we must increase the number of rules and managers and put more effort into planning.

However, Linux and *Wikipedia* prove the opposite is true. Rules and planning, that's the most pointless work there is. Instead, everyone should just go ahead, do what needs to be done and spend their energies on actual work. Planning creates *Nupedias* (and, according to Linus Torvalds, Hurd kernels), whereas the cheerful work that reminds you of an anthill produces the Linuxes and *Wikipedias* of the world.

This is particularly true when you factor in that not all planners are all that smart. Which means organizations risk having their entire staff doing something really inane, because that's what somebody planned. So, it seems better to have a little overlapping and lack of planning, because at least you have better odds for some of the overlapping activities actually making sense.

According to wiki philosophy most people can and want to do what's right – they actually want to do their best. Inhibiting this natural inclination with a plethora of rules and unnecessary checking procedures is rather more moronic than the limited amount of trouble caused by a small minority of

---

76 OK, so there ought to be an acknowledgement here for the source of this story, but I've managed to lose it. Surely a little thing like that shouldn't keep a guy from telling a good story!

aberrant 'ants'. And despite what that 20 per cent of ants do, every summer millions of parents take their children to admire an ant hill, not to criticize it.

Of course, *Wikipedia* does have rules which writers should follow. The most important rule puts the wiki philosophy in a nutshell: *If rules make you nervous and depressed, and not desirous of participating in the wiki, then ignore them entirely and go about your business.*[77]

The two years spent working on *Nupedia* were essentially a waste of time. Once bitten, twice shy, they say – but apart from the lesson of experience, there wasn't much else to take away from it. At the time of writing, *Wikipedia* has just turned three. So, how is it doing?

In the early days of *Wikipedia*, Jimmy Wales had the company of Larry Sanger, who was paid to work on *Wikipedia* for the first 13 months. This is an interesting detail, if you compare *Wikipedia* to Linux. Linus Torvalds spent about a year working alone on Linux before other programmers from around the world began little by little to produce an increasing share of the code for Linux. In both cases it took one person to get the process going and give them a shove in the right direction, after which they developed their own momentum and kept going.

If you happened to use *Wikipedia* in its first year, the subject you looked for often wasn't there, because nobody had yet written an article about it. In accordance with the wiki philosophy, the accidental surfer wasn't then greeted with an error message but instead with an empty field for text and a polite request for the person to write the missing article. Little by little the articles came together, though the quality of the entries varied. Some were written by kids in schools corresponding to junior high, writing in English which was not their mother tongue, while others were penned by learned professors. The voluntary nature of the work naturally influenced the articles. Early on, *Wikipedia* had a very comprehensive presentation on the headwords 'beer' and 'Linux'. The article on 'Microsoft Windows', on the other hand, presented as obviously important the emulators which enable a user to run Windows software on Linux! You might say that *Wikipedia* is an encyclopedia that is the way it is because of the people who write it and use it.

Today, *Wikipedia* has volunteer editors, so-called *Wikipedians*, in the thousands. In January 2002, i.e. when *Wikipedia* was a year old, a thousand articles were written or revised each day; in January the next year the number had doubled to 2,000 a day. At the time of writing, the number of

---

77   http://en.wikipedia.org/wiki/Wikipedia#Policies

articles is approaching 200,000 and in addition to that there are a total of 55 other-language versions of *Wikipedia*. For instance, there were already a hefty 3,200 articles in the Finnish *Wikipedia*.[78]

Interestingly, statistics show that in the summer of 2003, more people visited the *Wikipedia* website than visited the web version of the venerable *Encyclopaedia Britannica*. The comparison isn't quite fair, though, as the *Britannica's* articles are only available to paying customers, but it does confirm that the three-year-old *Wikipedia* is the most popular Internet encyclopedia. And Jimmy Wales is actually planning to challenge the *Britannica* on its home turf. In the near future we will see the release of *Wikipedia 1.0*, a selection of 75,000 articles both in print and available on CD-ROM.[79]

Whenever there is talk of *Wikipedia*, people often point out that the king of all dictionaries *The Oxford English Dictionary* was also an Open Source project of sorts. The first edition, published in 1928, listed more than 400,000 English words in twelve volumes. The editors worked on the first edition for a total of 54 years, allowing the first Chief Editors to have died before it was actually published.[80]

Apart from the sheer number of words, the reason for the drawn-out process was that much of the OED was written by a large number of eager volunteers who were interested in linguistics. They collected words from newspapers and fiction as well as in markets and the local pubs. The words and their meanings were then mailed to the Chief Editor, whose job it was to coordinate the project. One of the better-known volunteers was J.R.R. Tolkien (1892–1973), who is said to have laboured mostly with words beginning with the letter 'W'. (For your information, Tolkien fans, the entries for *warm, wasp, water, wick, wallop, waggle* and *winter* were

78   http://fi.wikipedia.org/

79   *Wired* magazine wrote about Jimmy Wales and *Wikipedia* in November 2003 <http://www.wired.com/wired/archive/11.11/opensource.html>. The article cites many other examples of using Open Source methods in various non-technical fields of human life. Some of them have been mentioned in this book, some not.

80   But please note that *The Oxford English Dictionary* is a *dictionary*, whereas *Wikipedia* and *Britannica* are *encyclopedias*. An encyclopedia aims to tell you 'everything you ever wanted to know', whereas the aim of a dictionary is to catalogue all the words of a language together with a guide to their pronunciation, etymology and meaning. A parallel project to *Wikipedia,* called *Wiktionary* (http://wiktionary.org), aims to produce a multi-language dictionary. At the time of writing, *Wiktionary* has been around for a year and the English edition has more than 30,000 entries, which is rather less than 10 per cent of the first edition of the OED.

originally by him, so now you can rush off and read some more Tolkien wisdom.) Another volunteer, William Chester Minor, was convicted of murder and continued to send in his contributions from prison. And a Mrs Caland in Holland is said to have remarked that she couldn't stand her husband's never-ending work on 'that wretched dictionary'.[81] Although the OED in its final published form was not available for free copying, it would seem that the hacker spirit of working has been around for a long time.

dmoz.org, open web page index and MozDex, open search engine

In addition to *Wikipedia*, a number of similar projects also deserve mention. Older than *Wikipedia* and *Nupedia* is the *dmoz.org Open Directory Project*, which is an Internet link directory.[82] The first and still most popular similar (closed) directory is an icon of the Internet, *Yahoo!*.[83]

In 1998 it looked like automated search engines had come to the end of the road. The then most popular search engine, AltaVista, couldn't cope with the explosive increase in web pages, rendering the search results more and more useless. The sheer number of web pages made it hard to find what you were looking for and the situation was made even worse by various advertising companies who had learnt how to abuse the key word directories of web pages to get to the top of the search results lists. The situation resembled the one we now have with e-mails: whatever one did, no matter how proper were the words used in the search, the top of the search results contained pornography and – well, mostly pornography, because Viagra wasn't known then.[84]

That meant that the future seemed to be more and more dependent on directories made by human effort, such as Yahoo!. This was the niche that Chris Tolles and Rich Skrenta came upon. To them it was clear that gathering the fast-growing Web into any sort of directory cried out for an

---

81 From *The Meaning of Everything, The Story of the Oxford English Dictionary* by Simon Winchester, quoted at: http://www.ralphmag.org/CI/oed.html and http://www.askoxford.com/worldofwords/oed/wordsearchers/?view=uk

82 http://dmoz.org/

83 http://www.yahoo.com/

84 Viagra didn't hit the market until 1998 (http://en.wikipedia.org/wiki/Viagra) and at least in the spam that fills my inbox, Viagra ads are the largest single group.

Open Source approach. So, in June 1998 they founded a project to do just that, and called it GnuHoo – it's a small world, isn't it – or open Yahoo!. Since it wasn't an official Gnu project, they did as Richard Stallman requested and changed the name to NewHoo. Later on, Netscape, which was one of Yahoo!'s competitors, dropped its own directory project and bought NewHoo to be the basis of its own portal and made it the Open Directory. It finally found a home at dmoz.org.

Dmoz, or NewHoo, was a success from the start. In the first month alone it had scored some 31,000 links, which 400 volunteer editors had organized into 3,900 categories. Only a week after that there were 1,200 editors and 40,000 links![85]

In the same year, 1998, AltaVista lost its position as the leading automated search engine and was slowly forgotten as the lead was taken over by a newcomer, Google, which thanks to a highly-developed PageRank algorithm could once again make some sense in the order of the search results. That also tipped the balance in the competition between automated search engines and edited ones in favour of the automated ones. However, it is worth noting that Google and many other search engines use dmoz as one source of information in the creation of their own database. So, whenever we use Google, we are in many ways using Open Source. First, the Google servers are based on Linux and Open Source code; and second, the Google search engine uses an Open Source source of information.[86]

Though the edited directories lost the fight to Google, the Open Source community didn't give up. In April 2004 a new contender joined the search engine competition: *MozDex.*[87]

MozDex is a perfectly open search engine. Not only is it based on Open Source code, but the intention is also for it to be open in the presentation of search results. How do we know that the search result Google lists first is really the best? Can we be sure there isn't some Google employee who has fiddled with the database or that they haven't sold the number one spot to whoever pays most? Even though we do trust Google, we cannot be completely certain. MozDex aims to provide search results that offer all

85   Wide Open News, 12.6.1999: 'License to search'.
     http://web.archive.org/web/20011108043741/www.wideopen.com/story/224-2.html

86   While Google servers are based on Linux and Open Source code, the Google code itself
     is top secret.

87   http://www.mozdex.com/

users the opportunity to check why the links which come highest on the list really are the most relevant. Next to each search result, there is an (*explain*) link, which allows you to see on what basis the given search result has scored higher than the other pages in the database.

In the words of the programmer of the MozDex search engine Doug Cutting, 'The number of Web search engines is decreasing. Today's oligopoly could soon become a monopoly, with a single company controlling nearly all Web search for its commercial gain. That would not be good for users of the Internet.'

At the time of writing MozDex is still an experiment and its database doesn't yet contain all the web pages on the Internet. But April 9 2004 will remain in history as the day Open Source joined the search engine competition. Google won the first round, but will Open Source make a comeback? That remains to be seen.

Books for schools, colleges, and cooks, other facts and some fiction

As with Linux manuals and encyclopedias, the content of school and university textbooks tends to be relatively easy to divide into sections, which makes them ideal candidates for being written by a variety of authors using the Open Source method. Schoolbooks are also an enticing field because teachers often produce their own material to use alongside the official textbook for the course they're teaching, particularly at universities. For some university courses a suitable book may not even exist, which makes the students entirely reliant on their lecturer's transparencies. Some courses also cover subjects that simply aren't found altogether in any one book, but rely on a variety of material being brought together from several different books.

What could be better suited to Open Source than that? If the books were free for teachers to use – and by 'free' I mean precisely the Open Source kind of freedom, free right to copy anything or change things – a teacher or lecturer could easily combine them to create a book perfectly suited to the curriculum being taught. The most relevant parts of each available book could be brought together, leaving out all unnecessary chapters, and if any chapters do not adequately cover what is necessary for a particular course the teacher could add to or even write their own versions of them. In fact, teachers already often do this, but instead of having a confusing hodgepodge of antiquated books, photocopies and handwritten notes, an Open Source system which allowed copying would enable teachers to compile a properly relevant course book, which could continually evolve and improve, and be updated whenever developments or newly acquired knowledge required new additions to be made.

Open Source course books would also be a good option for students. Towards the end of university studies, it's not impossible for a text book on some elevated technical subject to cost up to €200. An Open Source course book would naturally be cheaper for a publisher to print, just as Linux is cheaper than Windows. In the case of an Open Source course book, students could also elect to print the book themselves, or only the pages they actually needed, which would further bring down the cost of materials – not to mention save trees! In extreme cases a poor student could even read the whole book on the computer screen, for free.

With such compelling arguments for Open Source books, it would be odd if there were not already some on the Internet. But rest assured, they are there to be found. In the past few years the Internet has practically exploded with projects to write Open Source course books. Some projects are only at the idea stage, but others already have material on offer. There are projects that follow a given country's national curriculum, and others that are international, such as for English language teaching. For some reason even the State of California has its own project to produce schoolbooks for junior high school.

It's not easy to get a real overview of this embarrassment of riches for future schoolbooks, but it does seem that the wiki philosophy has once again proved its worth, because one of the most well-developed projects is *Wikibooks*, which is based on the *Wikipedia* code.[88] At least in its early stages, the project has so far focused on the production of textbooks, although it also includes a number of guides. At the time of writing, *Wikibooks* is only six months old but there are already dozens of more or less finished books in English, totalling more than a thousand individual chapters; and among the Finnish Wikibooks one book has already reached the *complete* status. It was a book under the heading Social Sciences entitled

---

88   http://wikibooks.org/

Työoikeus (Labour Legislation).[89] (Of course, in a wiki nothing is ever completed for ever; the *complete* status is more like the version number '1.0' of a computer program.)

And while we're on the subject, by the summer of 2003 *Wikipedia* had spawned quite a number of new projects. In addition to the *Wiktionary* and other *Wikibooks* projects already mentioned, there are also: *Wikisource*, a collection of open texts not originally produced through the wiki method (such as, the Bible, Greek philosophers, the US Declaration of Independence, etc.); *Wikitravel*, an open travel guide; *Wikiquote*, a collection of famous quotes[90]; and *Wikiversity*, a collection of university-level textbooks that uses *Wikibooks*.

But *Wikibooks* is by no means the only site for Open Source textbooks; the Internet is simply bursting with high-quality books. One of the most comprehensive directories in this area is *The Assayer*, which is maintained by Benjamin Crowell.[91] *The Assayer* is not a wiki, it's simply a link directory of open books available elsewhere on the Internet. In addition to the directory itself, the site also offers users a chance to assess and grade the books they've read.

Although in principle *The Assayer* lists any type of literature, it would seem that most open books are available in the fields we've covered. There are Linux manuals and textbooks. Among the textbooks, mathematics, physics and chemistry are by far the most represented, probably because of their close connection to information technology and therefore to Linux. The next largest group is actually fiction, which is pleasing in itself because it's not something we have to learn for school.

Benjamin Crowell also made his mark as a writer of Open Source course books by writing two series of university textbooks: *Light and Matter* and *Simple Nature*. Already *Light and Matter* – his series on introductory physics – is used as the course books in at least 17 universities. Everything suggests that Open Source literature really has something to give to future generations of students.

---

89   http://wikibooks.org/wiki/Työoikeus

90   For example: 'I live', Finnish author Aleksis Kivi; or 'They couldn't hit an elephant at this distance...', General John Sedgwick, Union commander in the US Civil War. Both quotes are among the Famous Last Words listed at Wikiquote, http://quote.wikipedia.org/wiki/Famous_last_words

91   http://www.theassayer.org/

And because education really is for life, and not the other way around, it's time to move on to everybody's favourite subject – food. The perfect companion to all the open Linux manuals is Matthew Balmer's *The Open Source Cookbook: Fuel for Geeks.*[92]

The book is probably of great use to young nerds who have recently moved into a place of their own and who are about to wake up to the reality of there no longer being a parent around to disturb their long coding sessions with calls to dinner. Because this cookbook really is aimed at nerds, there's a section before the actual recipes that lists what is needed before one starts to cook, which explains the need for basic equipment such as a pot, a microwave oven and a cutting board. After this, there's a run-through of the basic foodstuffs that should be found in every kitchen, even a nerd's; this is the list that takes you beyond coke and frozen pizza. There's also a brief glossary of techniques and terms, which explains the mysteries of having to julienne, knead or marinate.

After 'Cooking 101', the recipes are good enough even for a visit from mother. Members of the international hacker community really do share their best with you in the cookbook they have collaborated on at the Slashdot website.[93] So, what do you think of a gastronomic adventure that involves deep-fried kangaroo? Naturally, the recipe begins with information on which web stores non-Australians can turn to for kangaroo meat. Oh yes, nerds have the know-how!

Incidentally, *Wikibooks* also offers a cookbook, so the health of nerds should improve from here on. That is, if they remember to leave their computers every once in a while.[94]

Project Gutenberg

One project of great merit definitely deserves to be mentioned here for its archive of free literature. Project Gutenberg has on its server electronic

---

92   http://www.ibiblio.org/oscookbook/

93   http://slashdot.org/

94   http://wikibooks.org/wiki/Cookbook

versions of almost all the classics of world literature available for free distribution.[95]

Unlike in the computer business, which is still very young, a large number of famous works of literature are freely available for copying, publishing, and for distribution over the Internet because they have passed the time limit built into the copyright laws of various countries. Copyright protection lasts a specific number of years following the death of the author or creator of a work, after which it enters the public domain. The protected period of copyright varies from country to country and with the type of work it is, but it the usual period, depending on the country, is usually 50 or 70 years from the death of the creator of the work, or from the date of publication if it was published posthumously.[96]

Since there aren't many programmers who have died over a hundred years ago, the period of copyright is not something that has affected the development of computer programs, such as Linux.[97] But the situation with literature is quite different. Despite the extension of the copyright period, most of the literary classics are already in the public domain, which allows the Gutenberg archives to offer an extensive library of e-books, ranging from the philosophers of antiquity and various translations of the Bible, through Shakespeare's plays and *Moby Dick*, to *Alice in Wonderland* and *Peter Pan*.

---

95 http://www.gutenberg.net/

96 Here, the reader may like to know of a twist in the tale. Originally, the copyright period covered a considerably shorter length of time; in the US, for instance, the period was a measly 14 years. Mysteriously, that period has been extended to its current multi-generational length. Interestingly, new laws have been passed to prolong the period of copyright whenever the copyright for Mickey Mouse (first published in 1928) is close to expiring. Without the latest 20-year extension in 1998, Mickey would have entered the public domain in 2003.
http://writ.news.findlaw.com/commentary/20020305_sprigman.html
http://www.wired.com/news/politics/0,1283,17327,00.html
http://reason.com/links/links011703.shtml

97 Apparently, there are a total of three programmers who died over a hundred years ago: Joseph-Marie Jacquard (1752–1834), the Frenchman who invented a programmable loom in 1801 (http://en.wikipedia.org/wiki/Jacquard_loom); Charles Babbage (1791–1871) (http://en.wikipedia.org/wiki/Babbage), an Englishman who designed a 'difference engine' and an 'analytical engine', also in the nineteenth century; and his friend Ada Lovelace (1815–1852) (http://en.wikipedia.org/wiki/Ada_Byron), who wrote programs for the analytical engine, despite it never being built. Other nineteenth century mathematicians mulled over the creation of a programmable computer, but these three are typically cited whenever the prehistory of computers is mentioned.

Project Gutenberg was begun by Michael Hart as early as 1971, which as e-programs go makes it a really old one. At roughly the same time the UNIX operating system and the C programming language were taking their first tentative steps. It is actually quite amazing that there was even a computer for Michael to use for his project at this early stage. However, the University of Illinois had a computer, and Michael was one of the people to whom the university endowed some computer time.

The other people using the computer at the time mostly did very elementary work on it, such as programming a programming language. That's a bit like making the hammer which will eventually be wielded to make the scaffolding used to build the walls of a house, and only when the house is finished, will others finally get to decorate and furnish it – all quite comparable to cave dwellers discovering fire.

However, Michael Hart didn't want to get involved in such projects, and tried to come up with something else to do with his computer time. After all, at the time this was a resource that would have cost $100 million to buy! You couldn't exactly leave it unused.

Having thought about it for an hour and 47 minutes – so it is said – Michael Hart predicted that the greatest future value of computers would not be their calculating capabilities, but in storing information and in the unlimited distribution and search for information. Not a bad guess! Thus began Project Gutenberg, and the first information stored by Michael was the *US Declaration of Independence*, which being a public document was common property; that is, in the public domain.

The *Declaration of Independence* may not qualify for a place in the top ten of Western literature – particularly for non-Americans like myself – but it was more than nationalistic pride that made Michael Hart choose that particular text. There were actually some very practical concerns: it was suitably short, which meant it would fit it on the disks available in 1971. The time for storing the whole of *Moby Dick* and the *Bible* came later, as the technology developed.

By 2003, the Gutenberg archives included more than 10,000 e-books, which were published on a 4 gigabyte DVD to celebrate the achievement. The present aim of the project is to reach a million free e-books by the year 2015. Despite its modest beginnings, Project Gutenberg has shown what resources can be found in being free and by using volunteers.[98] The project's history also reminds us that the current boom in Open Source thinking isn't really anything new. As Richard Stallman keeps telling those younger than himself, the entire IT business was Open Source in the 1970s. The change to a more closed world came later. The same goes for e-books. Michael Hart was doing it in the 1970s, but it was the twenty-first century before Stephen King tried it.

Music

Although the Internet has also revolutionized the music business, most of the big headlines to date have been about Napster, its progeny and the delaying action record companies have been fighting against them. These so-called peer-to-peer technologies are revolutionary in themselves, but there's no denying that their users have crossed over to the wrong side of the law. It is illegal to distribute copyright-protected music over the Internet without permission from the copyright holder.

Even though Napster, which first made it possible for users to swap music files with one another, had to close shop after a court order, it has hardly slowed the sharing of MP3 files. Napster was simply supplanted by a handful of new technologies built in a way that made it impossible to close them down at one central server, as was done with Napster. The record industry, fighting to protect its rights and more importantly its source of revenue, hasn't yet given up what seems a hopeless struggle, but keeps on tossing this or that spanner into the works.

At the time of writing, the record companies have managed to make their already soiled image worse by, among other things, suing the twelve-year-old daughter of a penniless single mother from New York for having used a file-sharing program. Whereas, the companies selling file-sharing programs made themselves even more popular by paying the poor girl's $2,000 settlement with the industry. There was also an Internet collection to get the same $2,000 together. Somehow, it seems the record companies are very much alone in their fight.

---

98   Sources: http://www.gutenberg.net/about.shtml and
      http://www.upi.com/view.cfm?StoryID=20040106-041656-1684r

Last year a lot of artists added their own voices to the anti-record-label chorus.[99] Probably the most well-known of these is Moby, a big name in electronic music who has openly spoken in favour of file-copying fans.[100] He says he is genuinely happy that people want to listen to his music and if they can listen to it through file-sharing then that's fine by him. The way Moby sees it, a lot of his fans have actually first heard his music through files downloaded from the Internet, something that makes him happy rather than angry. In addition to Moby, several other musicians are rumoured to be feeding their songs into the file-sharing programs – which is quite contrary to what one would expect, judging from what the record companies say. The group Offspring said in a TV interview that they had even included some MP3 files as bonus material on their latest record but the record company had removed them before it was released.

Formerly of pop-dance duo Wham!, singer George Michael was the first major league pop star to announce that the record he released in the spring of 2004 will be his last.[101] The album concluded his deal with his record company and in future he will release all his new songs (of course, he has no rights to the old songs, which are the property of the record company) on his website, where fans can download them for free. There will be no charge for copying the songs, but anyone who wishes to do so can give a donation to one of the charities listed on the site.

The rocking granddads of Offspring are happy to talk big in interviews, lashing out against their greedy record-label masters, but sneaking your own MP3 files into file-sharing programs is not exactly Open Source. They may be angry that a signature on an old recording contract prevents them from putting their own songs onto their own website, and George Michael is certainly leading the way in this, but these are just the first steps. As far as I know, he hasn't agreed to hand out his music for others to profit from or to sell on the same terms as Linus Torvalds did with his Linux code.

But there are some real revolutionaries out there. A small record company called Magnatune states on its front page: *We're a record label.*

---

99 Rock star Courtney Love, for instance, accused the record companies of being the true pirates. See her article 'Courtney Love does the math' at:
http://dir.salon.com/tech/feature/2000/06/14/love/index.html

100 http://www.moby.com/

101 http://news.bbc.co.uk/2/hi/entertainment/3499534.stm

But we're not evil.[102] The owner John Buckman founded the company after seeing how his wife fared with a standard recording contract she signed with a traditional record company. About a thousand records were sold and his wife, as the recording artist, earned a staggering $45. As a result of the contract, she lost all rights to her own music for the next ten years, which means she cannot put the music she has written on her own home page despite the fact that the record has sold out and cannot be bought or reordered from anywhere. John wanted to found a record company that would offer recording artists a better deal.

The music recorded by Magnatune can be downloaded quite legally either a song at a time or as whole albums from the Magnatune website. In addition to which, the site can be used to create your own personal web radio broadcast by selecting the music you want to hear. (Even realizing such a technically simple and fun idea is practically impossible with traditional copyright practice.) Naturally, one can also order actual CDs from the company, because of course that is what a record company sells. The music available has grown relatively quickly and encompasses a broad range. There are now more than a hundred artists in the Magnatune camp, and the label has already released some 200 albums. It's good to see that different types of music are represented by Magnatune; in addition to the ever-present techno there's a lot of classical music and quite a nice collection of jazz.

Magnatune's music also passes the criteria for openness. Although a separate deal must be made and paid for to use the music commercially, all the music available on the website can be used for any non-commercial purpose according to the rules of Open Source. John Buckman uses the term *Open Music* to describe the principle. It means anyone can use the music as a background to their own film, or make their own version of one of the songs. Many artists actually make the 'source code' of their songs available with a view to this, meaning you can download midi files or given audio tracks. The only condition for reusing songs is that the use must be non-commercial and that the original artists must be acknowledged. And most importantly, the new work must be made available to other people under the same conditions.

This last 'ShareAlike' condition brings to mind Richard Stallman's copyleft principle, which most Linux programs use. On the other hand,

---

102 http://magnatune.com/

Open Source computer programmers have seen fit to ease up on the condition of non-commercial use. Because there are some actual costs to the distribution of programs – such as the price of a blank CD and postage – the criteria of non-commercial use didn't seem to further the aims of the GNU movement, which was to spread GNU software as far and wide as possible. History has shown that commercialisation didn't hurt Linux – quite the contrary. The other demands of openness included in Stallman's GPL licence have been enough to safeguard openness and fairness and prevented the creation of monopolies.

Although the conditions for Magnatune's music also include that of non-commercial use, the company's existence and work is a step in the right direction, particularly when compared to the exploitative capitalism of traditional record companies. Perhaps the requirement for non-commercial use is just an evil we have to live with during a transitional stage and something that can be discarded in the future.

The next step has actually been taken by a record company called *Opsound*.[103] The music available on the Opsound website is made freely available in any shape or form, there's only the ShareAlike clause to ensure the material continues to be free and open in the future. Which means the music from Opsound could be used in a film that is sold to a television channel, provided the television channel is given the same right to use the whole of the film in the same way and the channel commits to passing this right on to all its viewers. This model is beginning to look very much like the GPL licence which is used to sell Linux. So, it's looking good!

Statistics show that Opsound has yet to reach the same levels as Magnatune. The number of artists is roughly the same and the music files number around 400, but at the time of writing, the first record is only just being released. The music available through Opsound tends to lean towards machine music, but an interesting specialty is the recordings from various environments that might be best classified as sound effects rather than music. My own favourite is a piece called *Pildammsparken*, a recording from a Swedish bird lake.

I will end this review of the open music scene with the joyful piece of news I read some time ago in a small local paper of Pietarsaari, the town where I was born. A composer-cum-lyricist called Iiris Lumme had published a song book containing a hundred or so of her own songs, and the

103 http://www.opsound.org/

joyful thing about the news snippet was that she states categorically in the preface that 'all songs may be freely copied and sung; that's why they've been printed here.'

That is indeed why music has been made throughout the ages. But at some point we seemed to have forgotten this, and music became the property of record companies, which meant that artists and listeners have had to ask them for permission to enjoy what they like doing. The example set by Iiris is touching in that this old lady has probably never even heard of Linux and may not have a clue about what it means to share MP3 files over the Internet. To her it was just the natural way to publish her songs. They were written to be sung.

Iiris's openness has also brought her some modest financial success: I, for one, naturally rushed to order a copy of her song book, despite the fact that I'm not much of a singing man. And I suspect there are more people out there who'd like a song book like that – with songs you can sing!

Creative Commons and building an open infrastructure

Although some works akin to Open Source have been created in various cultural activities, there are still some challenges to be faced before the revolution reaches the proportions of Linux. These challenges might be termed problems of logistics. In the production of Open Source programs, such problems have already been solved, but in literature, music and the other arts, fitting solutions are yet to be worked out.

One hurdle still to be overcome in the Open Source revolution in the arts is the default position of all copyright law. It forbids everything. The logic of copyright is that all works of art have a creator, and that person owns all rights to their own work, unless they expressly cede them to someone else or, for instance, expressly give permission for them to be copied. In the past, under US copyright law it was assumed that a person's work could be used freely unless such a work had been expressly marked with the © symbol and thereby protected under copyright law. In other words, the maker had to expressly signal that their work was protected if that is what they wanted, otherwise it was assumed that the work could be freely used and distributed.

And although we are interested in freedom here, in principle the new copyright system is better. It protects creative people from greedy and exploitative people or companies, such as some music publishers, whose lawyers could – if copyright law still depended on use of the © symbol – probably come up with any number of technical violations in how the symbol had been used by an author, artist, or musician, and thereby allow corporations to take over a person's works without paying for the right to do so.

But there is a downside to this. The way things are now, one needs permission for everything. Finding a poem, an article, or a song you love on the Internet doesn't yet give you the right to use it in a work of your own. First, you need to get permission from its copyright owner (usually the author or publisher, or via the author's agent), and that can be difficult because few MP3 files, for instance, include the copyright holder's e-mail address or telephone number. So, a certain song may not get sung at a concert simply because it wasn't possible, without an inordinate amount of effort, to contact the copyright holder and ask for permission. At the same time, the world is full of artists like Iiris Lumme, who would love their songs to be sung, copied, and performed in concerts.

This makes it important for composers, authors and artists around the world to learn to take this difficulty into account in the same way Iiris did in the preface to her song book. Regular Joes like us who want to share our songs and words with others must learn to act within the framework of copyright law.

Computer programmers have learnt to do it when they write programs. The General Public License (GPL) developed by Richard Stallman has become the standard and that licence or a similar one is always mentioned at the beginning of any programming code. In just a few lines it immediately advises anyone reading the code that they are allowed to use it in their own programs. The GPL is recognized by Open Source programmers, and just mentioning it is enough to tell all and sundry that a code is free for anyone to share. Without such a mention the code could not be used – copying and using it would automatically be prohibited by law.

For the Open Source revolution to spread seriously into literature, music and the other arts, all originating artists and songwriters such as Iiris Lumme must learn to include a short GPL-like permission at the beginning of their works. That would immediately signal how the work can be used, and eliminate the need for others to seek permission to use it. If this habit were to become widespread, those who publish writing, photographs, or drawings on their websites could significantly influence the amount of material that can be used freely. All great waterfalls begin with small rivulets, don't they? From such rivulets the entire GPL'd Linux operating system was built.

The GPL has also been used in copyrighting books and music, but since the license itself specifically relates to computers and source code, this is not logical. Which is why similar licences, specific to their purpose, have been developed. A collection of licences under the *Creative Commons* brand has garnered the most publicity and the greatest number of users.[104] Some big names have supported this licensing, among them Eric Eldred, who publishes free literature such as titles from Project Gutenberg, and law professor Lawrence Lessig. (Together they opposed the latest extension of the period of copyright inscribed in copyright law in the US Supreme Court. They lost, but only by a whisker.) Creative Commons has also endeavoured to make its licensing options more widely recognized, so that artists themselves learn to add the (CC) logo to their work when they want to permit copying, just as programmers include the GPL reference in their codes.

On the Creative Commons website people writing for the desk drawer or composing their own songs can easily choose a licence that suits their particular work. The process requires almost no knowledge of law, and finding the right licence takes just a couple of clicks of the mouse. You can allow or prohibit the copying and distribution of your work for commercial purposes, or require that your name be included in the list of contributors to any work in which yours has been used. The notice used by Creative Commons is 'Some Rights Reserved', rather than the 'All Rights Reserved' conventionally included in copyright notices. If you want to make your work totally free, that is put it in the public domain, you can include a logo that bravely states 'No Rights Reserved'.

These days, more websites are displaying the logos of the various licences. Little by little, Creative Commons is becoming the GNU movement of the literary and arts world, and the (CC) logo its GPL licence.

In addition to aspects of the law, another logistical problem stands in the way of using free works of art, and that is how and where to find them. Over the years, web pages with tens of thousands of Open Source programs have grown up to help the Open Source movement. For instance, SourceForge is home to nearly one hundred thousand Open Source projects. Such umbrella indexes do not yet exist for literature, music and the other arts. Creative Commons has created their own search engine called Get Content, which

---

104 http://creativecommons.org/

looks for (CC)-licensed works. And those I mentioned earlier, Project Gutenberg and The Assayer, are also good reference sources. There is ongoing development in this area, so in the future finding free works will be even easier than it is today.

One of the difficulties of creating a viable system for finding works is the enormous size of the files. The code for a program is only text written by people, and though it is a huge job to collect tens of thousands of programs on one server, it is possible. Similarly, Project Gutenberg has amassed a lot of literature on its server, as books are merely large text files. Even photographs and other graphic works of art can be stored on a computer. However, music and particularly films take so much space on a hard drive that a wholesale storing of them in an index as well as distributing them through the Internet is technically challenging. Using the so-called broadband connections in use today, one three-minute pop song that has been packed as an MP3 file arrives within minutes, but you'd wait for several hours to receive a feature film packed in Xvid format. In reality, offering thousands of movies to be downloaded off the same server is not possible with today's technology.

Also, it needs to be considered that part of the Open Source philosophy is that it is not enough to supply the user with just the end product – a working computer program or a film to watch – but they should also be given the opportunity to take the work further in the same way as an original creator could do. This means that films couldn't be distributed in tightly packaged formats, but would need to be of at least DV quality. Another challenge is that all available raw materials should be available as well – and in a film that is typically tens or even hundreds of hours of film!

So, Creative Commons has managed to sort out the licensing problems, but we still lack efficient tools to find and distribute free works on the Internet. The traditional www server model may never be able to handle the distribution of several hours of video material. On the other hand, the peer-to-peer technology that has gained ground in the past few years – and which is now unfortunately mostly used for illegal copying of music and films – might just do. But who will create a Creative Commons version of Napster?

Here, it is good to remember that sharing simple computer programs wasn't easy in the 1980s either. The Internet was still in its infancy, few people had an online connection, and even for those who did it was so slow that anything bigger than an ordinary e-mail required a long wait. In those days, GNU programs were rarely distributed via the Internet but were sent on tape through the mail.[105] In fact, at the time, the mail order business of selling tapes with programs was an important source of income for Richard Stallman. So, despite the technical limitations of the Internet, there is no reason why films could not already be produced and distributed through the Open Source method.

Open Source movie night

We've already dealt with literature and music. So how about movies? I was about to write that the first Open Source film is yet to be made. But actually, one does already exist. The first and, for now, apparently the only feature film available under the Creative Commons licence is Brian Flemming's *Nothing So Strange*.[106]

This is a so-called indie (independent) film, produced on a small budget without support from any of the big Hollywood studios. Made in a fictional documentary style *Nothing So Strange* is about the investigation of the assassination of the world's richest man, Bill Gates. According to the press release, the plot resembles Oliver Stone's *JFK*, which similarly investigated the assassination of President Kennedy, the disappearance of evidence, the silence of authorities, and other twists of plot.

What a coincidence that the first Open Source movie is about the murder of Bill Gates, founder of the Microsoft monopoly and sworn enemy of Open Source software. And actually it is a coincidence, because the film wasn't originally planned to be Open Source. In fact, it was produced according to the traditional closed methods of filmmaking. At the time, Brian Flemming may not even have heard of Open Source.

In the end, the film distributors were not interested in the film and simply refused to take it on. Apparently a film that kills off a real and hugely influential person wasn't a plot they wanted to promote – or perhaps the film was just plain bad. I can't judge that, because I've not seen it.

---

105 Floppy disks were only coming into use in the 1980s and they used many incompatible standards. Also, the storage capacity of one floppy was next to nothing. CDs had yet to catch on.

106 http://www.nothingsostrange.com/

In order to keep the film alive, Brian Flemming released as Open Source the raw material used for the film. Considering the plot, you'd think that some Linux fans would have been interested in buying either a DVD of the actual film or, in a best-case scenario, actually have chosen to edit the film material into versions of their own, creating new endings and new twists to the plot.

Although this did give Brian Flemming's film some publicity, no Open Source movement ever really emerged around the movie. Nobody has made any alternative versions of the film and apparently nobody even ordered a copy of the DVD containing the raw material.

So, even though one Open Source movie does exist, I think I'm justified in saying that the first Open Source movie is yet to be produced. Without in any way diminishing Brian Flemming's valuable contribution to works licensed under Creative Commons, it's obvious that the great strength of the Open Source ideology is not in the publication of the final product, but in the open approach taken throughout the entire production process. Flemming has expressed interest in making a movie as Open Source from beginning to end. So, the cliffhanger now is, who will make history by being first to complete a genuinely Open Source movie?

Meanwhile, it's interesting to wonder what sort of film the first Open Source movie would be. What would distinguish it from the bulk of Hollywood productions that we can watch on television any night of the week?

If we start with the basics, naturally the film's screenplay should in itself be Open Source. It could be based on one of the classics available through Project Gutenberg, but it's more likely to be a story expressly created for the film. Lots of people would be involved in the scriptwriting process, cooperating over the Internet. Perhaps wiki technology could be employed in creating the screenplay?

Arranging the actual shoots, could be problematic for an Open Source film production, but would also provide interesting opportunities. Common to the Open Source method is that anyone, anywhere can get involved in creating or changing any given part of the product. In a film, this could pose a problem with the actors, at least those in the leading roles, who are usually the same people from beginning to end. It would be rather confusing if halfway through the movie the role of a character played by Richard Gere was suddenly taken over by Danny DeVito, only to have DeVito supplanted by the Finnish veteran actor Vesa-Matti Loiri!

To use programmer talk, the actor's person is not modular. You can't share a role among several participants. But in the future, perhaps this too will be overcome. The latter parts of *The Matrix* trilogy already had long fight sequences entirely done with computer-generated imagery (CGI). As computers evolve, it will be possible to take an accurate, three-dimensional, full-body scan of the actors, after which the film can be made entirely on computers while the actors themselves lie in the hot tub. As this technology becomes widespread, it will be possible for the movement and conversation of the characters to be shot anywhere, and anyone with the right skills will be able to do the animation, just as Open Source programming is done. Even today, that is already possible, if one is satisfied by making an animation feature such as *Toy Story*, *Antz* or the *Hulk*. In fact, such films could be made using Blender, the program I wrote about in the Third Part of this book.

In filmmaking, the Open Source approach would be particularly helpful in creating the special effects and animating the actors, because both these jobs demand an incredible amount of computing power. DreamWorks and the other Hollywood studios actually have so-called animation farms to do this work with thousands of super-fast computers all linked to one network. Their only job is to render the animated scenes, i.e. compute the finished image on the basis of the movements and other instructions given by the animator. Despite the enormous power harnessed to do the job, rendering is nonetheless slow work. It can easily take a whole night to render one scene, although with the simplest scenes one might get time for a longish coffee break.

Computer animation is ideal for the Open Source method of working. It would be perfectly possible to get thousands of volunteer Internet users to give processing capacity on their computers for the making of the next hit movie. There is already a lot of distributed computing being done. Popular topics for which distributed computing is used include the search for electronic messages in the omnipresent cosmic background radiation – in other words, extraterrestrial life.[107] In its search for suitable proteins to help find a cure, cancer research makes use of distributed computing.[108] And over

107 http://www.seti.org/science/setiathome.html

108 http://www.chem.ox.ac.uk/curecancer.html

700 personal computers are being used in the search for mathematical prime numbers.[109] The idea of distributed computing is to make use of the idle processing potential when our computers are switched on but doing nothing. Whenever a computer user is having a coffee, is out to lunch, speaking on the phone, or even reading a web page or writing an e-mail, most of the processing potential of their computer is not being utilised. The websites of the above projects allow willing computer users to install a program that will make use of that idle processing power on their behalf and send the results back to the server, which will then collate the results from all participating computers into a common database.

In 1999, an interesting result was generated by distributed computing when Distributed.net took part in a competition arranged by RSA Security to break an encryption based on the DES algorithm.[110] Distributed.net participated with a network of nearly 100,000 computers and broke the encryption in less than 24 hours. Curiously, the computing power of the volunteers of Distributed.net was more than double that of the $250,000 super computer that Electronic Frontier Foundation had built expressly for the purpose.[111] The DES Challenge clearly showed how strong the Internet fraternity is, even when it comes to raw computer processing power.[112]

If somebody wanted to use distributed computing to produce the special effects for a movie – no matter whether it was Open Source or a traditional Hollywood production – I'm quite sure millions would volunteer their

---

109 http://www.mersenne.org/
Find dozens more similar projects on: http://www.aspenleaf.com/distributed/

110 http://www.distributed.net/des/

111 http://www.eff.org/

112 The results of the DES Challenge also showed, and this was the main goal of the organizers, how vulnerable the DES encryption was, despite the fact that it was widely used and recommended by the US administration. RSA's competition finally forced the US to allow the export of stronger encryption systems than the DES.
Another interesting story regarding the ban against exporting heavy encryption programs is the PGP program developed by Philip Zimmerman. The hefty encryption methods of this program should also not have been allowed to leave the US according to the same law. Philip and his friends chose to publish the source code for the program on paper – 6,000 pages in 12 volumes. The books were flown to Europe, where they were scanned onto a computer and the source code was compiled into a working program again. The rationale was that you could not ban the export of books, because that would have been against the article of the US Constitution that guarantees freedom of speech. (http://www.pgpi.org/pgpi/project/scanning/)

computer power. Who wouldn't want to walk tall in a T-shirt saying, for instance: 'My computer powered special effects for *The Matrix*.'

But for the actor problem there is also another solution. What if the film had no main characters? Today, few films have many leading roles and often not many supporting roles either. Obviously, this is because actors are expensive, but an Open Source movie wouldn't have that problem. Volunteers around the world would be keen to get involved in making a film. So why not make a movie with tens or even hundreds of smaller leading roles? The number of extras could run into the thousands – as many as one could get to show up. It's been decades since Hollywood has produced a spectacle with thousands of actors, because it's too expensive. Today, all huge crowd scenes in films are computer generated by cloning a group of perhaps twenty or so into a sea of people thousands strong. But our Open Source movie would have no problems of expense. The more people involved the merrier! Just like with Linux.

So, what we want is a script that no Hollywood studio would agree to shoot. It could have dozens of characters and thousands of extras. The events would be set around the world, in the most exotic places imaginable, and there would be so many of them that no single film studio's travel budget would be able to realize it.

Once the film has been shot, using hundreds of actors and camera crews, it would need editing and post-production work. The available raw material would be shared over the Internet and, if necessary, participating 'filmmakers' would send each other material on tapes or DVDs by mail. The filmed material would be edited into vastly different segments in different parts of the world, and slowly evolve into the final film. The music for the film would naturally be distributed under the Creative Commons licence, and for sound effects there's the Opsound archives.

The resulting movie would be a true masterpiece. It would be a monument to the collaboration of hundreds of writers, composers, musicians, cameramen, actors, directors, wardrobe artists, builders, animators, and countless others.

But what would the film be about? What sort of plot would work for such a film, with hundreds of roles and locations? Ironically, one good idea for the storyline is the evolution of Linux and Free Software. After all, Free Software is created by very dissimilar people working in various parts of the world during all hours of the day and night. So what could be better than making a film about these people and their work using the Open Source method? Brian Flemming, if you're reading this, get in touch!

OpenCores – free hardware

Taking the Open Source ideology into literature and other creative areas is an obvious step, but there's yet another interesting question to consider. If software can be produced and distributed using the open model, then how about the hardware? If I can use Linux and other Open Source programs on my computer, when will the computer itself be as open as the programs running on it? In a sense, personal computers are an open architecture in the sense that you can build your own computer by using components that meet certain open standards. But today, the components and their production processes are in no way open.

Offhand, you'd think there's no way the open model could work for computer components – surely, what works for software can't work for hardware. The source code of programs, the text of a book, films and audio files all have one thing in common: information stored in digital form can be copied an unlimited number of times, for free. But computer components are tangible parts of the physical world, and here again we hit the traditional laws of supply and demand. Our empirical knowledge of the world says that one computer is one computer and as such can't simply be distributed by open methods.

But in fact, despite our empirical experience, there are projects working towards the manufacture of Open Source computer components. The most well-known of these, OpenCores.org, actually seems to be doing well and is even mass-producing some products for the computer market![113]

So what is this all about?

I don't understand about electronics any more than most people, but to go any further we'll need some knowledge about how integrated circuit cards are made.

Some components of a computer are the micro processor, various RAM memories, a modem or network card for connecting to the Internet, a card to connect the screen and another to bring sound to the speakers. All these various components are attached to the motherboard, which in itself is a

---

113 http://www.opencores.org

brilliant piece of electronics containing several microchips. Consumers assume these bits and pieces all come from a factory somewhere, packed into plastic and cardboard, and are eventually fitted together. To that is added a keyboard, a mouse, speakers, monitor and – Hey, presto! – we have a computer.

But in reality the manufacture of these microchips is a lot like programming – but instead it's called design. Actually, separate programming languages are used for designing microchips. The most popular languages are called VHDL and Verilog.[114] These descriptions of integrated circuit cards written in VHDL or Verilog are the really hardcore stuff. To be able to read them, you need to understand both electronics and programming, and all they tend to give a regular Joe like me is a headache. But those who understand this language are the people who make the microchips you and I use every day. And I'm not just talking about computers, because microchips are everywhere: in fridges and cars, in wood pulp factories and elevators.

Having the VHDL language files on a computer allows one to use a more or less automated process to manufacture a so-called gate-level description, then to use these logical gates to create the physical model, or layout, of the integrated circuit. The final stage is to make the mask (a sort of mould) which is used to radiate (or cast) small transistors and wires onto a silicon disk.

In this way the manufacturing line at the microchip factory is relatively automatic for making microchips from semi-conductor materials according to a blueprint. The chips are then packed and sent off to the computer manufacturer, the car plant, fridge factory, or wherever. Naturally, there's an art to building and maintaining a manufacturing line like that, and one essential is that these factories must be cleaner than an surgical operating theatre and be entirely dust free. There's a lot of other magic to the process, but we won't go into all that here. One time-consuming part of the work of designing an integrated circuit is the so-called timing. In this world of physics, one must understand that the electric signal in the circuit only moves with the speed of light – no faster. That's why a logical and accurately designed VHDL file won't generate a microchip that works as it

---

114 Who can keep track of all these acronyms? VHDL is short for *VHSIC Hardware Description Language*, and VHSIC itself is an acronym for *Very High Speed Integrated Circuits*.

should unless the electrical impulse actually reaches from transistor A to transistor B fast enough but not too fast.

For this general explanation, that is as far as we need to delve into that. We just have to believe that what it comes down to is that the data in a VHDL file is used to make a mould which is then used to make semi-conductor materials become a working microchip.

That means the major single effort in making a microchip goes into designing it. That takes a programmer who can write code in the VHDL language. Then testers are needed to check that the chip works as designed. Naturally, the testing too is done before a single chip is made, by creating a model of the VHDL file inside a computer program to simulate how the chip works. Testing is an extremely important part of the manufacturing of microchips and plays a far larger part in the design work than, for instance, in the writing of software, because it's a lot harder to fix a microchip after it's been made. So, microchips have to be virtually flawless before a manufacturing line is set up to produce them in the thousands.

This simplified explanation doesn't really hold true for all microchips. The fast processors like Pentium, Opteron or Athlon, which are made for new computers almost approach the occult, defying as they seem to do the laws of physics. But for those processors, too, design is the largest part of the job, after which making the fancy microchips is no different from making simpler ones. A great deal of fine-tuning of the production line and other hard work goes into squeezing the last ounce of effect out of these high-speed processors. Again, without going into detail, the challenge is to get as many transistors and wires to fit onto the semi-conductor as possible. And once the production line can be made to manufacture small enough transistors, the next task is to get the electrons that transmit the electrical signal to stick to the right wires. If the wires are too small and too close together, the electrical signals will hop from one wire to the next, everything gets confused, and the processor is useless.

That's the case for the newest and fanciest microprocessors. In contrast, as long as you're not out to set a speed record the manufacture of other processors is – so I'm told – very nearly as easy as I've described above. You take the finished VHDL file to a subcontractor who manufactures microchips, and moments later finished processors start popping out the other end.

Opencores received a lot of publicity in December 2003, when a genuine integrated circuit was made from its Open Source design.[115] Several manufacturers have now made the same chip, but the first, historical, Open Source chip was made by Flextronics Semiconductor, or the same company that makes chips for Nokia, of cell phone fame, and Cisco, which makes most of the routers for the Internet. This certainly proved that Open Source can work even in the components part of the computer business – in hardware as well as in software.

It's not as if the OpenCores chips would not have been realized much earlier as so-called FPGA chips.[116] Widely used in electronics because they are flexible, FPGA chips are also popular with OpenCores and others who design chips as a hobby or for teaching purposes. It's a sort of general-purpose microchip. It comes empty from the factory and users can 'load' it with whatever features they like, which they've first written in VHDL, for instance. The P in the acronym FPGA means 'programmable'. In making prototypes the FPGA chips are invaluable, because they are usually reprogrammable. Which means, once a user has tested their chip they can tweak their own VHDL code and reuse the same chip to try the new version.

To 'load' – or program, as the professionals say – an FPGA chip, a separate device is connected to a computer for the empty FPGA circuit to be plugged into. However, some FPGA circuits forget all they had contained every time the computer is turned off, and the chips have to reload each time it's turned on again. Actually, FPGA circuits could be compared to CD burners, which are now an integral part of all new computers. We all used to think CDs could only be made at a CD factory, but then somebody invented the CD burner and now anybody can burn a CD with their home computer. Naturally, a home-burned CD won't be of equal quality or as durable as those made in factories, so there's no point in making multiple copies of

---

115 'Open Source Finally Hits Real Silicon' was the headline on the website Slashdot, popular with geeks, on 8 December 2003:
http://slashdot.org/articles/03/12/08/2326236.shtml
For more about the chip itself, go to:
http://www.opencores.org/projects.cgi/web/or1k/silicon

116 Let's sort out this terminology: participants of the Opencores.org project seem to use the term FPGA widely to refer to any programmable microchip. Which is why it is also used in that sense in this section. In the name of fairness, let it be known that many engineers in this field think FPGAs are only one sub-group of programmable chips. For those interested to learn more, Wikipedia has the information at:
http://en.wikipedia.org/wiki/Programmable_logic_device

CDs at home. But thanks to CD burners any music lover can release their own CD if they want. Similarly, your average electrical engineer can make their own processors using FPGA chips.

And although you won't get the effect of a Pentium or Opteron using these general-purpose chips, a modern FPGA chip can already be used to create a microprocessor corresponding to the ancient 486dx. In plain language that means a computer as powerful as those used in the early nineties could be built by a handy electrical engineer entirely from Open Source components! The equipment necessary to program an FPGA chip isn't even expensive. For those interested, various development kits are available from a number of companies, such as Altera and Xilinx, and prices range from around €80 to several thousand. Of course, a really handy electrical engineer could also build the circuit board that is used to program the chip, in which case the whole process would cost next to nothing.

Open Collection – fashion, brands, and fabric

The achievements of the OpenCores project have opened up entirely new opportunities for using the Open Source method. The project has already demonstrated that Open Source thinking can be applied outside the virtual world. We've already dealt with computer programs, literature, music and films, and now OpenCores has taken Open Source thinking into the manufacture of tangible products. Does that mean Open Source can be applied to just about anything? Considering the products sold in stores and all the stuff we live with, it's clear that in the end many of them have very little to do with the possession and treatment of raw materials. Instead, many products have a surprising number of *intangible* characteristics that are well suited to the Open Source method. Computer programs and the intellectual content of books are intangible, which is why the notion of creating and distributing them through Open Source was so obvious. But a lot of intangible work also goes into the manufacture of other things, which is why almost any product can benefit in some way from Open Source thinking. At the beginning of this book, I used oil as an example of a raw material, a limited natural resource for which production and sales follow the law of supply and demand, a mean-spirited logic. However, Rob McEwen's story showed us that there are advantages to be gained from Open Source thinking, even when digging for gold. If such thinking can be used in gold-mining and in the production of microchips, surely it can also be applied elsewhere – even in drilling for oil.

For instance, let's look at clothing. Could clothes be manufactured using Open Source methods? Why not – particularly as programming was born out of a loom.[117] It is clearly time to reunite computer programming and the production of clothes, although this time it is the world of fashion that has something to learn from the hackers.

Clothing is a good example of an everyday product, but that doesn't make clothes mundane or unimportant. If you don't believe me, just ask the next teenager you happen to meet.

When it comes to buying clothes, it's not just about the garments themselves. First of all, there's the *brand*! Many people would rather buy a very expensive pair of Nike sneakers because the brand has high status on the street, than buy a cheaper unbranded pair, even of equal quality. To maintain the high status of their brand, Nike pays Tiger Woods hundreds of millions of dollars to be their public showcase, yet they pay the Asian workers who make the sneakers just a couple of dollars a day.

Of course clothes – like microchips – are also about *design.* Today, when people talk about making clothes the sewing itself may never be mentioned, but more likely they'll discuss the coordination of cut, fabric and colour – the design. And if we're talking about sneakers – say, Nike sneakers – the designs are created by engineers like myself, because today's sneakers really are masterworks of engineering. They include so many special features, such as soles with air pockets and ventilation holes for perspiring feet, that just taking a walk has become an equipment sport. Once the design is decided, the actual manufacture of footwear or clothing is a minor detail, and the main focus becomes where it can be done most cheaply. Which is why so many clothes are made in Asia, by people who work for a couple of dollars a day.

But that's not the end of the story. Once the Asians have been good and sewn a big pile of clothes or shoes, these need to be delivered to stores in Europe and the Americas, and that is a matter of logistics. And – apart from the trucks, ships and aeroplanes – logistics are mostly about information technology.

---

117 As I stated in an earlier footnote the first *programmable* machine, and therefore the forefather of all computers, is reckoned to be the loom invented by Frenchman Joseph Marie Jacquard in 1801: http://en.wikipedia.org/wiki/Jacquard_loom

Brands, design, logistics, project control, and so on, are intangible and therefore areas in which Open Source methods are strong. But how is an Open Source clothes brand created? In order to understand that step, we must look to Richard Stallman's General Public Licence (GPL) and the principles behind it. In addition, we need tools that make sharing easier, such as SourceForge or BitKeeper, which Linux programmers use in their work. And then, of course, we need designers, seamstresses, makers, and shopkeepers – all sorts of people to do all sorts of things – just like in Linux. And because it's all about creating a brand, we also need a name. Let's give our clothes the brand name *Open Collection*.

Open Collection is a clothes brand that lets *anybody* take part in its creation. Anybody, from children to grandmothers, from students of design or the arts to the best-known designers in the fashion world. Anyone who wants to, can create sewing or knitting patterns, textiles, pictures, logos, and anything else that is part of designing clothes. Their patterns are stored on a www page on the Internet and are available for others to use. Naturally, everything is done with some form of the GPL type of licensing, so that anyone is free to use any of the patterns or textile designs so long as they too contribute their own changes for others to use.

Just as a working computer consists of several smaller programs, a single piece of clothing consists of several separate design elements. One person or company may have developed the fabric; someone else may have created the pattern printed on it; and a third person may have combined the colours in a new way. Yet another person designs the cut of the garment and determines how its seams will look, while a fifth designer decides on the shape of the pockets, and so on. Like many other jobs, making clothes is often a collaborative effort. And collaboration is what Open Source is good at.

Just as there are several Linux distributors, there would surely be many manufacturers of Open Collection clothes. And why not? If you could get fashionable designs free off the Internet and there was a demand for the clothes, then the manufacturers would definitely be interested. And just as Linux is different to Microsoft, so would an Open Collection be different to existing brands of clothes, in that nobody would own it. It would be our common brand. An Open Collection manufacturer in Asia might take the initiative to produce these clothes, but would have to find themselves a European importer or store to sell them. Not having to pay expensive licensing fees to the owner of the brand would in theory allow the manufacturer to pay more to their employees who actually make the clothes. In addition to large-scale clothing factories, there would also be manufacturing on a small-scale. Teenagers could sew their own fashion clothes if they chose, and grandmothers could knit Open Collection sweaters. Some people would make their own clothes to save money, others because they enjoy doing it, but most people would continue to buy their clothes from the stores because they have things they prefer to do, other than sew clothes – just like with Linux. Some people would buy clothes made by the cheapest manufacturer, while others would prefer to buy clothes made in their own country or perhaps handmade clothes – just like with Linux. In schools and colleges, people doing craft- or needlework classes could make their own Open Collection shirts and print them with images of their own choice in their art class. Or they could just print out images they like. And nowadays, special paper for making transfers is available for inkjet printers. Images printed on it can be ironed onto, for instance, a T-shirt. See how much we engineers have done to enable people in the clothing business to take the Open Source revolution to its next stage.

The quality of the Open Collection brand clothes might vary slightly. While uneven quality is usually considered bad, here the diversity would be a feature of the Open Source process used to create the clothes. It is unlikely that any two shirts, each made by a different manufacturer, would ever be completely identical despite their design having originated from the same pattern. One manufacturer might make it in a Mexican cotton fabric while the other one makes it with linen from India. And each homemade shirt from the same design would also be unique. And that is just the way we like it. Open Source is all about the joy of doing, of appreciation for individual makers, and of celebrating versatility!

Something else that differentiates Windows from Linux is that Windows is made by a company, whereas Linux is made by individuals. This is a significant difference which those who have switched to Linux are usually very excited to discover. When a computer user encounters a problem with a program made by a faceless corporation, they must call that corporation's technical support. Usually what they get is an answering machine that tells them to press 1 if you have this problem, press 2 if you have that problem, and press 3 if you want to speak to a human being. If they make the mistake of pressing 3, what they get is a pre-taped message telling them that 'unfortunately all our lines are busy at the moment, but please hold and wait for your turn'.

Whereas, if you encounter a problem in an Open Source program you can tell the makers of the program about it directly by e-mail. The e-mail address is always given in the source code of the program, and is even easier to find on the 'About' page of the program. The makers are usually very happy to have your feedback and answer you with thanks because you have told them how they can improve their program. If the corporation behind a closed program even answered an e-mail informing them of a flaw, it would probably come from a company lawyer denying the existence of the problem.

So a label on an item of Open Collection clothing would not, for example, say 'Made in Hong Kong', but in the spirit of Open Source would read something more like: 'These sneakers were sewn by Lu from Shanghai, the design was by Fabrizio from Brazil'. And if they'd also included the seamstress' e-mail address, a buyer happy with their new pair of sneakers could even send Lu a brief note of thanks. At the same time, he or she could ask about Lu's working conditions and make sure that all the employees were getting decent wages and that no child labour was used in the manufacture of the shoes. In these ways, Open Source could even help to address the problems about which the movement against globalization has been voicing such loud concerns in recent years.

Garment manufacture is just one example of the many business activities that could benefit from the adoption of Open Source thinking. However, this book is now written and the as-yet-unwritten innovations of openness will continue to grow out of the ingenuity and imagination of people who see the advantages of Open Source methods. We have seen how Open Source thinking can change the world of gold mining, encyclopedia publishing, and the clothing industry, and I hope such examples will encourage people to develop and innovate in ever more inventive ways. I am convinced that the stories presented in this book are just the beginning, and that there is plenty of room for a new generation of innovators like Richard Stallman and Linus Torvalds.

How about restaurants publishing their secret recipes on the Internet for customers to make at home? The recipes would be freely available for use by other Open Source restaurants who similarly publish their own recipes on the Internet for others to use. Customers could add their own favourites to the collection and, for instance, order their own favourite dish as made by the best chef at a five-star restaurant. The restaurants could have a common menu and a common logo and brand. It would be an Open Source chain of restaurants – perhaps called *McOpen*.

Yes, yes. There are plenty of ideas to go round, particularly when one gets excited. It's been exciting for me, at least, to relate these stories. I hope they've enthused you, too, because enthusiastic excitement is one of the greatest virtues of the hacker community. I hope their stories will inspire all of us to think and behave more openly – to live an open life.

Epilogue

While this book was being prepared for its original publication in Finland, an essay written by Linus Torvalds himself turned up within the files of the Linux source codes. In his essay he explains the management culture that developed over the years in the kernel project. On 10 October 2004, Linus added the file into the Linux kernel sources as a file *Documentation/ ManagementStyle* and labelled the addition as 'Wisdom passed down the ages on clay tablets'. Hidden within the source codes of the kernel the writing has not received much publicity, but it embodies so much life experience and wisdom, that it should definitely be compulsory reading for any corporate manager. In it we witness the silent nerd turn into a brilliant psychologist and leader, sharing what he has learned while working successfully for 13 years as the project manager for one of the world's largest software projects. And I can't think of a better way to end this book than giving the final word to the master himself.

Linux kernel management style, by Linus Torvalds[118]

This is a short document describing the preferred (or made up, depending on who you ask) management style for the linux kernel. It's meant to mirror the CodingStyle document to some degree, and mainly written to avoid answering (*) the same (or similar) questions over and over again.

Management style is very personal and much harder to quantify than simple coding style rules, so this document may or may not have anything to do with reality. It started as a lark, but that doesn't mean that it might not actually be true. You'll have to decide for yourself.

Btw, when talking about "kernel manager", it's all about the technical lead persons, not the people who do traditional management inside companies. If you sign purchase orders or you have any clue about the budget of your group, you're almost certainly not a kernel manager. These suggestions may or may not apply to you.

First off, I'd suggest buying "Seven Habits of Highly Successful People", and NOT read it. Burn it, it's a great symbolic gesture.

(*) This document does so not so much by answering the question, but by making it painfully obvious to the questioner that we don't have a clue to what the answer is.

Anyway, here goes:

Chapter 1: Decisions

Everybody thinks managers make decisions, and that decision-making is important. The bigger and more painful the decision, the bigger the manager must be to make it. That's very deep and obvious, but it's not actually true.

The name of the game is to _avoid_ having to make a decision. In particular, if somebody tells you "choose

---

118 Originally published in a file named *ManagementStyle* in the Linux source codes *Documentation* directory. Linus added it there on 10 October 2004 with an annotation 'Wisdom passed down the ages on clay tablets'. Also published on LWN at *http://lwn.net/Articles/105375/*

(a) or (b), we really need you to decide on this",
you're in trouble as a manager. The people you manage
had better know the details better than you, so if they
come to you for a technical decision, you're screwed.
You're clearly not competent to make that decision for
them.

(Corollary:if the people you manage don't know the
details better than you, you're also screwed, although
for a totally different reason. Namely that you are in
the wrong job, and that _they_ should be managing your
brilliance instead).

So the name of the game is to _avoid_ decisions, at
least the big and painful ones. Making small and non-
consequential decisions is fine, and makes you look like
you know what you're doing, so what a kernel manager
needs to do is to turn the big and painful ones into
small things where nobody really cares.

It helps to realize that the key difference between a
big decision and a small one is whether you can fix your
decision afterwards. Any decision can be made small by
just always making sure that if you were wrong (and you
will be wrong), you can always undo the damage later
by backtracking. Suddenly, you get to be doubly
managerial for making _two_ inconsequential decisions -
the wrong one _and_ the right one.

And people will even see that as true leadership
(*cough* bullshit *cough*).

Thus the key to avoiding big decisions becomes to just
avoiding to do things that can't be undone. Don't get
ushered into a corner from which you cannot escape. A
cornered rat may be dangerous - a cornered manager is
just pitiful.

It turns out that since nobody would be stupid enough to
ever really let a kernel manager have huge fiscal
responsibility _anyway_, it's usually fairly easy to
backtrack. Since you're not going to be able to waste
huge amounts of money that you might not be able to
repay, the only thing you can backtrack on is a
technical decision, and there back-tracking is very
easy: just tell everybody that you were an incompetent
nincompoop, say you're sorry, and undo all the worthless
work you had people work on for the last year. Suddenly
the decision you made a year ago wasn't a big decision
after all, since it could be easily undone.

It turns out that some people have trouble with this approach, for two reasons:

- admitting you were an idiot is harder than it looks. We all like to maintain appearances, and coming out in public to say that you were wrong is sometimes very hard indeed.

- having somebody tell you that what you worked on for the last year wasn't worthwhile after all can be hard on the poor lowly engineers too, and while the actual _work_ was easy enough to undo by just deleting it, you may have irrevocably lost the trust of that engineer. And remember: "irrevocable" was what we tried to avoid in the first place, and your decision ended up being a big one after all.

Happily, both of these reasons can be mitigated effectively by just admitting up-front that you don't have a friggin' clue, and telling people ahead of the fact that your decision is purely preliminary, and might be the wrong thing. You should always reserve the right to change your mind, and make people very _aware_ of that. And it's much easier to admit that you are stupid when you haven't _yet_ done the really stupid thing.

Then, when it really does turn out to be stupid, people just roll their eyes and say "Oops, he did it again".

This preemptive admission of incompetence might also make the people who actually do the work also think twice about whether it's worth doing or not. After all, if _they_ aren't certain whether it's a good idea, you sure as hell shouldn't encourage them by promising them that what they work on will be included. Make them at least think twice before they embark on a big endeavor.

Remember: they'd better know more about the details than you do, and they usually already think they have the answer to everything. The best thing you can do as a manager is not to instill confidence, but rather a healthy dose of critical thinking on what they do.

Btw, another way to avoid a decision is to plaintively just whine "can't we just do both?" and look pitiful. Trust me, it works. If it's not clear which approach is better, they'll eventually figure it out. The answer may end up being that both teams get so frustrated by the situation that they just give up.

That may sound like a failure, but it's usually a sign
that there was something wrong with both projects, and
the reason the people involved couldn't decide was that
they were both wrong. You end up coming up smelling
like roses, and you avoided yet another decision that
you could have screwed up on.

Chapter 2: People

Most people are idiots, and being a manager means you'll
have to deal with it, and perhaps more importantly, that
they have to deal with _you_.

It turns out that while it's easy to undo technical
mistakes, it's not as easy to undo personality
disorders. You just have to live with theirs - and
yours.

However, in order to prepare yourself as a kernel
manager, it's best to remember not to burn any bridges,
bomb any innocent villagers, or alienate too many kernel
developers. It turns out that alienating people is
fairly easy, and un-alienating them is hard. Thus
"alienating" immediately falls under the heading of "not
reversible", and becomes a no-no according to Chapter 1.

There's just a few simple rules here:

  (1) don't call people d*ckheads (at least not in public)

  (2) learn how to apologize when you forgot rule (1)

The problem with #1 is that it's very easy to do, since
you can say "you're a d*ckhead" in millions of different
ways (*), sometimes without even realizing it, and
almost always with a white-hot conviction that you are
right.

And the more convinced you are that you are right (and
let's face it, you can call just about _anybody_ a
d*ckhead, and you often _will_ be right), the harder it
ends up being to apologize afterwards.

To solve this problem, you really only have two options:

  - get really good at apologies

  - spread the "love" out so evenly that nobody really

ends up feeling like they get unfairly targeted.
Make it inventive enough, and they might even be
amused.

The option of being unfailingly polite really doesn't
exist. Nobody will trust somebody who is so clearly
hiding his true character.

(*) Paul Simon sang "Fifty Ways to Lose Your Lover",
because quite frankly, "A Million Ways to Tell a
Developer He Is a D*ckhead" doesn't scan nearly as well.
But I'm sure he thought about it.

Chapter 3: People II - the Good Kind

While it turns out that most people are idiots, the
corollary to that is sadly that you are one too, and
that while we can all bask in the secure knowledge that
we're better than the average person (let's face it,
nobody ever believes that they're average or below-
average), we should also admit that we're not the
sharpest knife around, and there will be other people
that are less of an idiot that you are.

Some people react badly to smart people. Others take
advantage of them.

Make sure that you, as a kernel maintainer, are in the
second group. Suck up to them, because they are the
people who will make your job easier. In particular,
they'll be able to make your decisions for you, which is
what the game is all about.

So when you find somebody smarter than you are, just
coast along. Your management responsibilities largely
become ones of saying "Sounds like a good idea - go
wild", or "That sounds good, but what about xxx?". The
second version in particular is a great way to either
learn something new about "xxx" or seem _extra_
managerial by pointing out something the smarter person
hadn't thought about. In either case, you win.

One thing to look out for is to realize that greatness
in one area does not necessarily translate to other
areas. So you might prod people in specific directions,
but let's face it, they might be good at what they do,
and suck at everything else. The good news is that
people tend to naturally gravitate back to what they are

good at, so it's not like you are doing something
irreversible when you _do_ prod them in some direction,
just don't push too hard.

Chapter 4: Placing blame

Things will go wrong, and people want somebody to blame.
Tag, you're it.

It's not actually that hard to accept the blame,
especially if people kind of realize that it wasn't
all your fault. Which brings us to the best way of
taking the blame: do it for another guy. You'll feel
good for taking the fall, he'll feel good about not
getting blamed, and the guy who lost his whole 36GB
porn-collection because of your incompetence will
grudgingly admit that you at least didn't try to weasel
out of it.

Then make the developer who really screwed up (if you
can find him) know _in private_ that he screwed up. Not
just so he can avoid it in the future, but so that he
knows he owes you one. And, perhaps even more
importantly, he's also likely the person who can fix it.
Because, let's face it, it sure ain't you.

Taking the blame is also why you get to be manager in
the first place. It's part of what makes people trust
you, and allow you the potential glory, because you're
the one who gets to say "I screwed up". And if you've
followed the previous rules, you'll be pretty good at
saying that by now.

Chapter 5: Things to avoid

There's one thing people hate even more than being
called "d*ckhead", and that is being called a "d*ckhead"
in a sanctimonious voice. The first you can apologize
for, the second one you won't really get the chance.
They likely will no longer be listening even if you
otherwise do a good job.

We all think we're better than anybody else, which means
that when somebody else puts on airs, it _really_ rubs
us the wrong way. You may be morally and intellectually
superior to everybody around you, but don't try to make

it too obvious unless you really _intend_ to irritate
somebody (*).

Similarly, don't be too polite or subtle about things.
Politeness easily ends up going overboard and hiding the
problem, and as they say, "On the internet, nobody can
hear you being subtle". Use a big blunt object to hammer
the point in, because you can't really depend on people
getting your point otherwise.

Some humor can help pad both the bluntness and the
moralizing. Going overboard to the point of being
ridiculous can drive a point home without making it
painful to the recipient, who just thinks you're being
silly. It can thus help get through the personal mental
block we all have about criticism.

(*) Hint: internet newsgroups that are not directly
related to your work are great ways to take out your
frustrations at other people. Write insulting posts with
a sneer just to get into a good flame every once in a
while, and you'll feel cleansed. Just don't crap too
close to home.

                    Chapter 6: Why me?

Since your main responsibility seems to be to take the
blame for other peoples mistakes, and make it painfully
obvious to everybody else that you're incompetent, the
obvious question becomes one of why do it in the first
place?

First off, while you may or may not get screaming
teenage girls (or boys, let's not be judgmental or
sexist here) knocking on your dressing room door, you
will get an immense feeling of personal accomplishment
for being "in charge". Never mind the fact that you're
really leading by trying to keep up with everybody else
and running after them as fast as you can. Everybody
will still think you're the person in charge.

It's a great job if you can hack it.

Index